A LIFE OF JESUS

A LIFE OF JESUS

by
Shusaku Endo

Translated from the Japanese
by
Richard A. Schuchert, S. J.

PAULIST PRESS
New York/Ramsey/Toronto

Library of Congress
Catalog Card Number: 78-61721

ISBN: 0-8091-2319-3

Interior Design: Nancy Dale Muldoon

Published by Paulist Press
545 Island Road, Ramsey, N.J. 07446

Printed and bound in the
United States of America

CONTENTS

Preface to the American Edition 1

Translator's Preface 3

1. Farewell to the Daily Life
   of Nazareth 7

2. Near the Dead Sea 18

3. Perilous Beginnings 29

4. Springtime in Galilee 41

5. Spies 55

6. "The Son of Man Has Nowhere
   To Lay His Head" 69

7. Jesus the Ineffectual 79

8. Judas the Dolorous Man 89

9. "Jerusalem! Jerusalem!" 102

10. The Night of the Arrest 113

11. Men Who Sit in Judgment 129

12. "Into Thy Hands, O Lord,
    I Commit My Spirit"........................143

13. The Question 156

PREFACE TO THE AMERICAN EDITION

My book called *A Life of Jesus* may cause surprise for American readers when they discover an interpretation of Jesus somewhat at odds with the image they now possess.

Jesus as I depict him is a person who lived for love and still more love; and yet he was put to death, for he chose to live without violent resistance. My way of depicting Jesus is rooted in my being a Japanese novelist. I wrote this book for the benefit of Japanese readers who have no Christian tradition of their own and who know almost nothing about Jesus. What is more, I was determined to highlight the particular aspect of love in his personality precisely in order to make Jesus understandable in terms of the religious psychology of my non-Christian countrymen and thus to demonstrate that Jesus is not alien to their religious sensibilities.

The religious mentality of the Japanese is — just as it was at the time when the people accepted Buddhism — responsive to one who "suffers with us" and who "allows for our weakness," but their mentality has little tolerance for any kind of transcendent being who judges humans harshly, then punishes them. In brief, the Japanese tend to seek in their gods and buddhas a warm-hearted mother rather than a stern father. With this fact always in mind I tried not so much to depict God in the father-image that tends to characterize Christianity, but rather to depict the kind-hearted maternal aspect of God revealed to us in the personality of Jesus.

If my American readers will keep this point of view in mind as they move through *A Life of Jesus*, they will (I believe) gain deeper insight into just where the religious psychology of the Japanese and other Orientals coincides with their own, and they will better appreciate those points at which the two psychologies perhaps diverge.

1

The career of Jesus as it is presented in this book does not include the image of Jesus as the One who fulfills the Jewish Old Testament. On this point I agree to the dissatisfaction expressed by many theologians and clergymen. Furthermore, because I have written the book in my profession as a novelist, it contains no theological interpretations of the prophetic messages contained in the Bible. These interpretations lie beyond the design of the book in an area to which my competence does not attain.

As I assert near the end of the book itself, I do not think that my portrait of Jesus touches on every aspect of his life. To express what is holy is impossible for a novelist. I have done no more than touch the externals of the human life of Jesus. I do feel, however, that my work will not have been a waste of time, if only the image of Jesus that I (a Japanese) have touched can also strike a spark of vital appreciation of Jesus even in readers who have had no previous contact with the Christian religion.

Finally, I pray that my discussion of the execution of Jesus will not occasion the least displeasure for religious Jews. I am aware of the age-old controversies, even in academic circles, about whether it was the Jews or the Romans who killed Jesus. As an outsider I am not in a position to fix the blame on either side. The only point I desired to make is that Jesus was put to death by people whom he never ceased to love.

Shusaku Endo

Tokyo
Good Friday 1978

TRANSLATOR'S PREFACE

THE name Shusaku Endo will not be familiar to most Americans. A number of his books have been published in English translation, but so far only two have appeared in the United States. Endo himself was born in Tokyo in 1923. At the age of three he was taken by his family to the city of Dairen (Manchuria). Unfortunately the parents were divorced, and the mother (to whose memory Endo has always been devoted) moved back to Japan with her two sons, to live with a sister in Kobé. Following her sister's example, she became a fervent, strict-observing Catholic, and then, with the encouragement of both aunt and mother, Endo himself was baptized. He was eleven years old.

A few years later, questionable health saved the young man from military conscription, but it did not exempt him from the rigors of civilian war labor. By 1949, however, he managed to graduate in French literature from Keio University (Tokyo); he published articles on literary criticism and theory and did editorial work for various periodicals. In 1950 Endo was presented with the opportunity to study modern French Catholic literature at the University of Lyon. He spent three years in France, not always happy, and in the end he was hospitalized. After that, he survived two more long periods of hospitalization, with drastic surgery. (Hospital scenes abound in Endo's fiction.)

Before returning from France, Endo had determined to be a novelist on his own, and he had discovered the theme that runs through his serious novels: the failure of Japanese soil to nurture the growth of Christianity. Apparently this theme is an extrapolation of the author's own interior conflict.

A Life of Jesus, this work of non-fiction, stands in a pivotal position between the author's earlier serious novels and his later more optimistic ones. To cite only those titles which have already appeared, or will appear, in English translation, the serious works include *Silence* (a story of Christian martyrs and apostates during the ferocious Japanese persecution in the 1600's), *Yellow Man*, *Volcano, The Sea and Poison, Near the Dead Sea,* and a drama called *The Golden Country*. The later novels, which contain some comic episodes mingled with their pathos, include *The Wonderful Fool, The Girl I Cast Away,* and *When I Whistle*. In these latter stories the main characters are apt to be Christ figures—in that image of Jesus dear to the heart of Endo himself: innocent persons, vulnerable and ineffectual, who suffer at the hands of those whom they love, and eventually exert a mysterious spiritual influence.

Christianity has not flourished in Japan, even though the long history of this island country is a story of importing foreign ideas and ways: the Japanese writing system, Buddhist religion and Confucian ethics, industrial technology, democracy, etc. Yet always the people have maintained their distinctive Japanese character. Creatively they adapt whatever is adopted from abroad.

Christianity, however, has not been adopted. Why not? Joseph Kitagawa, a noted Christian scholar, is of this opinion:

> In sharp contrast to Confucianism and Buddhism . . . Christianity has tended to reject not only all the rival religious systems but also the values and meanings of the cultural and historical experience of the Japanese. . . . Christianity tends to make Japanese Christians *uprooted*—but not necessarily *liberated*—from their social, cultural, and spiritual traditions and surroundings. [Italics added]

Endo's theory—that Japan has not accepted God because God has been presented too frequently as an authoritative father-image—merits our consideration. The Japanese have a traditional saying to the effect that the four most dreadful things on earth are "fires, earthquakes, thunderbolts, and fathers."

Paradoxically the feminine mother-love image of God appeals to the Japanese, living as they do in a social order that is even now to a vast extent under male domination, where men retain reverential affection for their mothers, who—at least ideally—forgive and suffer and sacrifice for love of their children.

This book, therefore, must be read for what it is—a personal appreciation of Jesus written by a Japanese novelist, who is himself a Christian and who speaks to his non-Christian countrymen. Endo is very Japanese when he emphasizes the maternal image of God. He is a professional novelist in the way he is highly selective about choosing episodes in the Gospel narrative, which he then structures into a dramatic presentation of Jesus' life and death. He is a true Christian believer in the final chapter of his book, the mystery of Christ's resurrection.

All literary translation implies the interpretation of an original text and the re-creation of its substance and emotional impact in another language medium. My aim has been to produce a straight translation. I have not changed the substance in any way to "adapt" the material to what I imagine might be the needs or the expectations of Occidental and Christian readers. I hope this somewhat exotic book will bring a certain freshness to an already familiar story. Those of us who have no trouble about believing in the divinity of Jesus may come to a sharper vision and warmer appreciation of Jesus our brother, a human being who shares the pain of living with each of us, forever.

The translation is mine, but in reading the Japanese text I had the invaluable assistance of Mr. Francis Masahiro Urushibata. Father Eugene LeVerdiere S.S.S. was generous in reading the manuscript and was most helpful in identifying those biblical scholars whose names lay well disguised behind the Japanese syllabary. Finally, a word of thanks to Mr. Donald Brophy of Paulist Press for his always constructive comments, and to John Carroll University for continuing support in my study of Japanese literature.

Richard A. Schuchert, S.J.

Kamakura, Japan
April 1978

1 FAREWELL TO THE DAILY LIFE OF NAZARETH

WE have never seen his face. We have never heard his voice.

We do not really know what he looked like—the man called Jesus, of whom I propose to speak. Countless pictures of Jesus have been painted from imagination in accord with a conventional formula: long hair falling to the shoulders, the trimmed beard, the lean face with high cheekbones. Most artists have followed for centuries this traditional recipe in constructing their portraits of Jesus, each of them going on from there to suffuse the facial features of Jesus with the ideals of piety peculiar to the artist's own historical milieu.

Still, in the first days of the Church the face of Jesus was never fashioned to this mold. The early Christians had a certain hesitant reserve about trying to depict the faces of holy persons. Consequently, the craftsmen of that era did not address themselves to picturing the face of Jesus in realistic fashion. They portrayed "the Lord" by means of symbols—a fish or a lamb, a shock of wheat or a tendril of grape. In the age of the catacombs Jesus appears in the guise of a young man, fashioned in the Greek style, with the beardless face of an adolescent, quite different from the conventional modern image. After some years, however, beginning in the fifth century, the influence of Byzantine art determined the model of the face of Jesus which has persisted into our own day. By studying these portraits we can learn how mankind through its long spiritual history has come to visualize in the highest degree of purity and beauty the physiognomy of the holiest person who ever lived.

No one has actually seen the face and form of Jesus except for the people who lived with him, the people whose lives he crossed. Even the New Testament in narrating the life of Jesus gives hardly a hint concerning his physical appearance. Yet by reading the Gospels we are able to bring to our own mind's eye a lively impression of Jesus, thanks to the people who did get to know him and then were unable to forget him the rest of their lives.

Since the New Testament tells us next to nothing about the face of Jesus, we are left with no other choice but to rummage our own imaginations. According to Stauffer, the Jewish religion of that time required of any man who preached the word of God that he be "a person tall in stature and well put together." Stauffer claims that a man falling short of this description would not be warmly received but would become an object of criticism. If Stauffer's explanation is correct—and since the Gospel record nowhere indicates that people ever condemned Jesus for his external appearance—then Jesus very likely was a man of normal stature for a Jew. From there we go on to think of him as looking like other Jews of ancient Palestine, parting his dark hair in the middle and letting it fall to the shoulders, growing a full beard and mustache, with the customary beard, the customary hair style, and his clothing probably the worse for wear, as we surmise from the Gospel of Mark where Jesus allows his disciples to possess only the usual "sandals, but not a second coat." So much for the outward figure of Jesus, as far as painstaking imagination can piece it together.

The name Jesus—more precisely Jeshouah—was a common name found everywhere. According to the Jewish historian Josephus, author of the *Jewish Antiquities*, so many men bore this name that it came to lack all individuality. During his brief span of life, therefore, Jesus had nothing in his name or in his looks to distinguish him. He was ordinary, appearing in no way different from the mass of men who had to sweat for a living.

In the Gospel of John (8:57) people seeing Jesus one time said to him that he was not yet fifty years old, whereas he was in fact only in his thirties. Their remark is open to various interpretations, one possibility being that Jesus did look older than his years. Any appearance of premature age might well have been a shadow of nameless suffering which always played across his face, or perhaps his weary eyes reflected interior pain.

Presuming as much, we then can ask: When did this uncommon glow begin to hover in his eyes? The life of every man and woman who touched his own became eventually his burden. Did the process already begin from the days when he plied his carpenter's trade in the town of Nazareth?

Nazareth of Galilee is the town where Jesus grew up. In our own day it stirs to the hubbub raised by the tourists and by the hucksters who live on their purchases. The town lies surrounded by hills bearing olive orchards and cypress trees and many umbrella-shaped pines, but a steady gaze at the hustle and bustle within the town reveals on every side the misery of human existence: barefoot beggar children, and beggars blind and crippled, and the dingy little squeezed-in shops and houses lining either side of the up-and-down streets that are filthy with slop. The Gospel of John records how people in the old days had a saying that "nothing good comes from Nazareth" (John 1:46), and in the days of Jesus the place was nothing more than a back-country town of no particular interest to the Jews, for the living standard of the people there was even lower than it is today. The dwellings of the common folks were smeared on the outside walls with whitewash, but on the inside they were dingy as any cellars, with only a single window. There still exists in Nazareth today a number of houses similar to those ancient ones, to help us imagine the sort of house in which Jesus lived.

Because his foster-father Joseph was a carpenter, Jesus also learned that trade. Jews of that time had the custom of wearing something to symbolize their line of work—a dyer, for example, would wear a piece of colored cloth, or a public scribe a quill pen. So Jesus, too, most likely wore somewhere on his person the piece of wood to indicate his being a carpenter. We use the word "carpenter," yet the work did not consist in putting up buildings and houses, and it would be more precise to speak of Jesus as a cabinetmaker. Moreover, since most of the carpenters in Galilee were itinerant workmen, Jesus carried on his trade not in any established workshop, but rather by moving about in Nazareth and its environs according to demand. When we read in the Bible the parables related by Jesus, we gather a keen sense of how Jesus himself was acquainted with penury and the hardship of making a living, and how he knew first-hand the smelly sweat of men and women who work. His story of the woman who searched all over the house for a mislaid silver coin might very well have been based on something that happened in his own family. The woman in another parable, who put some leaven into three measures of meal, might well have been his mother Mary.

The Gospels say nothing concerning the death of his foster-father, but oral tradition holds that Joseph died when Jesus himself was nineteen years of age. On the supposition that he died while Jesus was still in Nazareth, we are led to think that Jesus then assumed responsibility for the support of his mother. It is not clear how many other children were in the family. Certain Protestant scholars, depending on Matthew 13:55 and Mark 6:3, claim that he had four brothers named Joseph, James, Simon, and Jude, along with several sisters. The Catholic side, however, holds that Jesus had no siblings, since the Hebrew words *ach* [brother] and *achot* [sister], the words employed by Matthew and Mark, can just as well indicate "cousins," in accord with the common usage of both these words throughout the Middle East. The Hebrew language in fact has no one word to denote specifically a cousin. In any event, until Jesus was somewhere between thirty and forty years of age he labored for his daily sustenance, living in the company of close relatives and sharing with them what was for all practical needs a single extended family.

What Jesus met every day on his workman's beat was not limited to life's grinding poverty. Miserable cripples and sick people appear one after another in the New Testament, and these misfortunate ones lived everywhere around Nazareth. The region is notable for extremes of daytime heat and nighttime cold, on account of which in ancient times many succumbed to pneumonia in that season of the year when the wind blows from the east. Outbreaks of dysentery were common, and especially in those parts adjacent to the Lake of Galilee and the River Jordan malaria also was recurrent. The descriptions in the Bible of people "possessed by an evil spirit" or being "a victim of high fever" most likely indicate people sick with malaria.

In summertime many people were bothered with eye trouble caused by the combination of flying dust and the intense ultra-violet sunlight. Victims of leprosy, too, appear in the Bible, and the lepers gathered together and shaved their heads, and were forced to live apart from any town or village. The most pitiful thing about their lot was not their being quarantined, but the way in which society abhorred the lepers for being stricken unclean as a punishment from God.

Blessed are the poor in spirit,
　for theirs is the kingdom of heaven.
Blessed are they that mourn,
　for they shall be comforted.

The words are those which Jesus later quietly spoke to the people on a hill in Galilee. Yet what a gap lay between the wretched realities of Nazareth and this vision of the "kingdom of heaven" which he so vividly proclaimed. God was still not about to endow the poor with heaven on earth. God was still not offering comfort to the wailing sick. Was God preserving silence toward the suffering of these forsaken people? Or then and there did some impenetrable mystery lie deep inside what appeared externally so wretched?

To me it is unthinkable that questions like these failed to stir within the heart of Jesus during his years at Nazareth. On every page of the Gospels we see an image of Jesus trying to share in all the sorrows of misfortunate men and women. One woman had suffered for years with her illness (referred to as an issue of blood), and when she merely touched his person with the tips of her trembling fingers, it was Jesus who felt the unhappiness which had been the woman's lot through half a lifetime. Weeping men and women—it is they who need consoling. Words to that effect, spoken on the mountain in Galilee, portray the basics of what Jesus sought from God. In his carpenter days at Nazareth, Jesus more than anyone already felt the gap which lay between the nature of his prayer and the hard facts of daily living. And simply because he felt as he did, his face seemed little by little to be growing older than the faces of his cousins. From time to time a look of anguish hovered around his eyes. This itinerant workman on his rounds of Nazareth and its vicinity suffered gnawing hunger of the soul. The heart of Jesus was chronically in need.

On the shore of the Lake of Galilee, not too far from Nazareth, lay the winter resort town of Tiberias. King Herod Antipas owned a villa there, and the town's style of life was designed for the affluent set. Roman customs prevailed there, all quite alien to the likes of Jesus.

The era under discussion is the time when Palestine was a vassal territory close to the eastern frontier of the great Roman Empire. Galilee, along with a section of land to the east of the Jordan River, was controlled by King Herod Antipas, whose authority was sanctioned for the time being by the Roman emperor. Rome had a legate in Syria and a governor in Judea, both under orders to keep an eye on the tetrarchs among whom the dependent territory had been parceled out; and so long as these petty kings maintained their fealty to Rome, they were recognized in their rights to a certain autonomy and to the maintenance of their armed retainers.

The lord of Galilee, King Herod Antipas, was one of the sons of King Herod the Great, a man who had aped the manners of the emperor himself while being astute enough not to ruffle the pride and the religious sensibilities of the Jews. Antipas, his son, managed in turn to maintain his own position by being more a sycophant to the Roman emperor than even his father before him. So it was that Antipas rebuilt a certain town in Perea and named it Livias (also Julias) in honor of the wife of the Roman emperor Augustus; and when Tiberius ascended the imperial throne to succeed Augustus, he then built another town in the Roman style on the west shore of the Lake of Galilee and named it Tiberias.

The inhabitants of Galilee did not look with favor on the enthusiastic Romanizing of King Herod Antipas. Quite the contrary, they watched his cultural assimilation and political servility with an eye of hostile discontent. The population of Galilee was heterogeneous in origin, but the people had been homogenized through their stalwart adherence to the Jewish faith. They nursed their xenophobia and maintained their scorn for the customs and the religion of Rome, which posed a threat to the purity of Judaism. From time to time their resentment of Rome broke out in plain rebellion, to the point were passion came in to generate an anti-Roman terrorist party known as the Zealots, of whom I shall speak later. Roman governors whom the emperor dispatched to Judea were ever in fear of the possibility of insurrection breaking out among the crowds of Galileans who came on pilgrimage to the temple for the religious festival of Passover.

The New Testament has nothing explicit to say about the extent to which Jesus, growing up in Nazareth, was affected by this traditional Galilean sentiment. But we can detect a scent of antagonism between Jesus and King Herod Antipas, the man who will afterward interrogate him in Jerusalem—the pervading atmosphere of hostility between true Galileans and anyone tainted by Greco-Roman manners. From the Gospels I get the impression, however vague, that in his travels from place to place Jesus always avoided the cities built by King Antipas.

The life-style of the opulent class in Tiberias was alien to Jesus, who was himself no more than a carpenter at Nazareth. He had no social contact with the world of those (including King Herod Antipas) who were so deep into Greco-Roman fashions and ways of thought. On this point Bornkamm's exposition is correct, where he says that "we can find in the thinking of Jesus no trace of any influence from the alien Hellenistic way of life."

But popular resentment in Galilee was not aimed exclusively against King Herod and the affluent class, for many Galileans were disgruntled also with the priestly caste in Jerusalem, which maintained its privileged position only by coming to terms with the empire of Rome. People suspected that priests like these were a contamination to the purity of Judaic religion. I intend to write more later about how all these sentiments of the Galileans then came to be magnetized in the person of Jesus.

From their tender years the common folk of Galilee, like Jews everywhere, were exposed to hearing read aloud by their elders that basic criterion of Jewish life and mentality which is the Law, or

Torah. When lads grew into young men, they joined their voices with the adults in the Jewish synagogues in reciting also from the prophetic books and from the psalms. Jesus in his days at Nazareth followed the life-style of the class of people to which he belonged. Together with them he experienced fully the stinking sweat, the misery, and the penury of the working class, and in the synagogue together with them he read from the various books of the Old Testament.

In brief, Jesus in his outward style was simply a young carpenter who cut no special figure in the town of Nazareth. Even his name was a commonplace one, and his life followed an uneventful routine no different from others. He was distinguishable only in his face, which appeared to be old beyond his years, and in his eyes, which at times betrayed a tinge of anguish, but only in such a way that no one else knew what lay deep hidden within his heart. . . .

In the fifteenth year of Tiberius, emperor of Rome, there appeared in the wilderness of Judea, a bleak desert lying south of the holy city of Jerusalem, the flaming figure of a prophet clothed in animal skin fastened with a leather belt. He is the man known in history as John the Baptist. Tradition says that John was born in Ain Karim, seven kilometers southwest of Jerusalem, of the priestly caste of the tribe of Levi, and that on reaching adolescence he disappeared into the wilderness.

For years on end the Jews had been waiting for "the prophet" to appear. In its root meaning the term "prophet" signifies a person entrusted with the word of God, and originally it did not denote a person who predicts the future.

It is difficult for modern readers to appreciate the religious feeling that prevailed in those days. For a long period the Jewish people lived perforce with their native land being dominated by foreigners, and their humiliation engendered in them a fierce ethnic pride. In all their national adversity and frustrations, never for a moment did they cease clinging in faith to their distinctive deity Yahweh, maintaining a profound sense of hope in the Messiah (Savior) whom Yahweh was going to send to them.

The national territory, which had never been very extensive, had been kept in subjection for more than five hundred years, first to Persia, then to Greece, then in turn to Egypt, Parthia, and Syria, and finally to Rome. Under all these foreign hegemonies, under different forms of oppression, the nation stubbornly refused to yield an inch on two points. One point was their religion, faith in their God Yahweh. The second was their near absolute trust that Yahweh would in his good time send them a national Messiah, in the image of King David of old, a Savior to restore again for all of them the territory and the national honor of Judah Their monotheistic faith in Yahweh had been under continual threat from neighboring nations and from the polytheistic religions of their conquerors; yet in every crisis they succeeded in preserving their faith, thanks to those prophets who defied the alien religions and to that part of the nation who obeyed the prophets. The title "prophet," as I have said, designates a person entrusted with the word of the Lord God (Yahweh), and that is the sense in which the title was applied to any leader who delivered zealous admonitions to the Jews on those occasions when they were in danger of being corrupted by the religions and the public morals of the foreigners.

The prophets interpreted the wrath of God and his vengeance, and with vehemence they urged the people to repent—the natural result being that the prophets themselves were inevitably persecuted by the establishment prevailing at the time. The prophets claimed that national honor and glory would be restored to the Jews, that the "kingdom of God" was coming. Yet in reality the kingdom of God had failed to materialize, and for more than five hundred years the Jews were forced to behold their land subjected to the barbarous Gentiles. In spite of all, however, the painful hopes and aspirations of the nation had persisted into the days of Jesus himself. An impassioned lamentation from the psalms clearly expresses this feeling of the Jews:

> Lord, where is thy steadfast love of old,
>   which by thy faithfulness thou didst swear to David?
> Remember, O Lord, how thy servant is scorned;
>   how I bear in my bosom the insults of the peoples.

In the fifteenth year of the Emperor Tiberius, suddenly a rumor spread that in the desolate wilderness of Judea, by the lower reaches of the Jordan River close to the Dead Sea, the long-awaited prophet (John) had finally appeared. Hearing the rumor, people had reason to recall a certain text familiar to them from the Book of Isaiah:

The voice of him that crieth in the wilderness,
"Prepare ye the way of the Lord,
Make straight a highway for our God. . . ."

John had appeared in the wilderness, just as the text said, and the style of his preaching went like this:

"You brood of vipers! Who warned you to flee from the wrath to come? . . . Even now the axe is laid to the root of the trees, every tree therefore that does not bear good fruit is cut down and thrown into the fire."

The voice of John was crying that the promised kingdom of God was close at hand; therefore, repent! The message reached Jerusalem of course, but it also carried as far away as the towns in rustic Galilee, including the town of Nazareth. The cry had its unmistakable appeal for the Galileans with their stalwart belief in Jewish religion and their hatred of foreign intruders. They had witnessed the inroads made by Roman ethics and religion into their own particularistic world. Heathen shrines and other buildings in Roman style had been erected in cities like Tiberias and Julias, and their own ruler, Herod Antipas, obsequiously pursued these fashions. Even the priestly caste in charge of the temple in the holy city of Jerusalem were living in compromise with Rome. The honor of the nation was under threat from within, and their religion was starting to corrupt at its very hub. These were the feelings of the common folk of Galilee in their day-by-day existence. The warning issued by John the Baptist drew their hearts like a magnet.

Among those who traveled to the wilderness of Judea to listen to the message of the prophet were certain fishermen from the Lake of Galilee. They had heard how John carried out a special rite called baptism, which he administered to the people gathering by the River Jordan.

It was probably around January of the year 28 by the Western calendar when Jesus of Nazareth determined to leave his family and his trade in order to join the religious community of John. We don't know the exact age of Jesus at the time. Luke 3:23 says in effect that "Jesus . . . was about thirty years old," but Luke may have employed that choice of words because being thirty years old was considered the ideal time of life by Jews in the ancient world. It is a turn of expression often used in the Old Testament—that "David was thirty years old when he was made king," or that "Ezekiel was thirty years old when called to be a prophet." I think myself that Jesus was somewhere into the decade of his thirties by the time he left Nazareth.

The Gospels give no direct evidence concerning the extent to which at the time of his leaving home he may already have been aware of the mission which lay ahead of him, yet Jesus was moved in his decision to forsake the life of Nazareth by detecting in the voice of John the Baptist something that appealed to his heart. Jesus had his own ideas about what was wanting to the Jewish religion as it was administered by the priests and the Pharisees in Jerusalem. Certainly it was spiritual hunger which brought him to decide to leave his mother and his numerous kinfolk. It is not so certain, however, that his decision won the amiable consent of the family, especially not the consent of his male cousins. In the straitened circumstances of the extended family it was no easy thing for them to lose the contribution from Jesus just when he was at the peak of his productive years. His mother Mary, or at any rate his cousins James and Joseph, Simon and Jude and the others, were not always completely in sympathy with him. Did their failure to understand Jesus have its beginnings right here? The kinsfolk also failed to see what lay beneath that shadow of pain which showed from time to time in the eyes of Jesus. Mark 3:21 and John 7:5 record explicitly how for a long time his kindred bore scant respect for him. From their point of view the shadow perhaps revealed no more than his being an irresponsible dropout from the world of reality—a man with the will to desert an established living at Nazareth and be off to the barren wilderness of Judea.

2 NEAR THE DEAD SEA

In our own day we can see the cultivated fields and the orchards of the *kibbutzim* in land lying close to the Jordan River, along which Jesus the carpenter from Nazareth walked alone in January of A.D. 28, intent to hear the preaching of John the Baptist. Yet even today, where the cultivated land comes suddenly to an end, we enter a bleak and baffling region. As one drives a car through the brilliant sunlight, the only things to strike the eye are wave on wave of hemispherical hills, a vast expanse of cracked and wrinkled earth. This barren valley of the Jordan continues on until the rider finds himself in Jericho, one of the oldest cities in the world. Jericho is blessed with water springs and palm trees, but the road beyond the oasis enters the brownish wilderness of Judea, an expanse of rust-tone mountains bearing not a single tree, not a single blade of grass.

South through the lonely valley moved the solitary figure of Jesus the carpenter. He walked alone. He knew the nature of the wilderness of Judea, in which he chose to live. It might well be called the end of the earth. Bald mountains lay on the horizon line like so many rusty skull pans. The wilderness stretched to the Dead Sea without a living creature save for the scant shrub or thornbush scattered here and there. The Dead Sea itself, in which swims not a single fish, lay wrapped in eternal silence, its lifeless surface reflecting a mirror image of the mountains of Moab where between one bare mountain and another the action of the elements had molded those precipitous cliffs that tower above the dry stream beds called "wadi."

Dreadful heat attacks the place in summer. Silence envelops the place at night, when not a creature stirs where the crags and the canyons lie crouched in the impervious gloom.

This wilderness of Judea for the Jews was a fearsome zone of terror, but it was also to them a fitting place for thinking about God, a place for being alone, a place for meditation. The wilderness also served as a place of hideout for outlaw rebels, and it eventually became a military stronghold fashioned by revolutionaries. The devoted members of the Essene sect built a monastery here, where for many years they carried on their rigorous ascetical life, aloof from oppression by the religious establishment in charge of the temple in Jerusalem. Some years after the death of Jesus, when the Jewish nation rose in rebellion against the Roman yoke, this wilderness became the nation's final military bastion. Furthermore, the idea was prevalent, in accord with prophetic passages in the Bible, that some day a prophet would emerge from this same wilderness to deliver an alert to the nation.

Three days of travel, it seems, would bring Jesus to the town of Jericho—close to the lowest point on the face of the earth, 840 feet below sea level—the city to which some 3,200 years ago the Jews eventually found their way in searching for the land of Canaan after their exodus from Egypt. According to the Book of Joshua, the Jews attacked the town and slaughtered the population brutally, putting everyone to the sword with no distinction being made for young and old or men and women. Then the Jews rebuilt the city and settled there, for the place had springs of water and groves of palm trees, in contrast to the inhospitable desert of Judea immediately behind them.

Most likely Jesus entered Jericho, from where he could see with his own eyes, not far away, the crowds of people assembled at the bank of the Jordan River, all of them waiting to be baptized by the prophet, and where Jesus himself at length joined the crowd to gaze at the austere figure of John and listen to his words. Then Jesus too was baptized at the hand of the prophet.

This special rite called baptism was not an established rite in what can be styled the main current of Judaism—not among the Sadducees, who derived from the social class of the priestly nobility, nor among the Pharisees, whose roots were more plebian. The ones who did practice baptism, particularly as their own peculiar form of initiation, were the devotees of the Essene sect, the group who led an eremitical life here in the wilderness of Judea after having been shooed away by the mainstream sects.

Who precisely were the Essenes? The New Testament bears no mention of this segment of Judaism. The Essenes were, as I said, an exclusivist group opposed to the Sadducees and the Pharisees, who were in turn engrossed in protecting their own vested interests in both the temple itself and in a deliberative governing assembly called the Sanhedrin. The Essenes, driven off by the establishment, pursued their life of prayer and stringent mortification here at the end of the earth, on the shore of the Dead Sea, where with a vengeance they kept watch for the coming of their own Savior Messiah.

The New Testament, for whatever reason, devotes not a single line to the Essene sect, but thanks to Josephus, the Jewish historian of the Roman period, all succeeding generations have been aware of its having existed.

> On the west side of the Dead Sea . . . lives the sect of the Essenes. Being in quarantine, they are the strangest people in the world. They have no women, they keep no money, their staple food consists of dates.

Our present detailed knowledge of the Essenes comes from the dramatic discovery of the Dead Sea Scrolls in 1947. In that year a shepherd boy belonging to a Bedouin group in the area was searching for a sheep gone astray from the flock, when he happened to set foot inside a cave on one of the mountainous crags near the shore of the Dead Sea in the wilderness of Judea. By sheer chance the lad stumbled upon some pottery jars, inside of which were discovered a number of manuscripts made by the Essenes. Archeologists, by excavating, discovered then in the same neighborhood the ruins of a "monastery" or community center. The excavated site is commonly referred to now as the Qumran Monastery. From these discoveries has come our knowledge concerning the sect of the Essenes, their way of life, their organization, and the religious teachings within the Qumran community.

Scholars began at once to speculate about a possible connection between the Essenes and the religious community of John, the man from whom Jesus received baptism. The scholars urged a number of points common to John the Baptist and the Qumran community of the Essenes: the same geographical sphere of activity, the same mysticism of the desert, the same asceticism, the same predictions regarding God's judgment, and especially (by conjecture) that John had adopted his rite of baptism from the Essenes, since the Qumran community also used baptism for their initiation rite. Of course, it is too much to leap from these considerations to any positive assertion about whether John the Baptist himself was a member of the Essenes. We cannot deny, however, a heavy Essenian coloring in the character of John.

Scholars next conceived of a connection between the Essenes and Jesus himself. The Dead Sea Scrolls include writings about a leader of the Qumran group known as the Teacher of Righteousness. This Teacher of Righteousness was both founder and director of the community, and he was persecuted and put to death by the Jewish religious establishment. The representative persecutor is referred to as the Lion of Fury, and the scrolls go on to relate how the Teacher of Righteousness was sentenced to be crucified by the priest called the Lion of Fury—all reminiscent of Jesus. It is even claimed that the Qumran devotees developed an idea that their founder (again like Jesus) would rise from the dead. (There are scholars indeed who reject this account of the founder's execution and the point about resurrection.) Because of the amazing parallel between the two stories there are certain scholars like Dupont-Sommer, daring enough to proclaim that the Teacher of Righteousness and the Christ are one and the same person.

There are points of similarity also between this particular religious community and the primitive Christian community. First of all, the Qumran community spoke of themselves as "the poor," and as

"the New Covenant," appellations identical with what the early
Christian community called itself. Second, both communities resembled each other in promulgating a system of common life in
which the members donated all they possessed to the group as a
whole. In the Qumran community, however, the common own-
ership of all property was of obligation, whereas with the primitive
Christian Church the donation was always purely voluntary. Third,
both groups made baptism the badge of their believing members,
although the baptism of the Qumran community should be understood as being merely a ritual ablution which does not include the
essential meaning of being born to a new life, as the term is understood in Christianity. In other words, the Essene practice of repeat-
ing one's baptism every year stands at odds with the Christian
practice of receiving baptism only once, and that for life. (We also
find scholars who advance a theory that Jesus and his disciples
observed the Passover and other religious festivals according to the
calendar followed by the Qumran community.)

At present, of course, we do not side with those whose spec-
ulations have leaped to identifying Jesus himself with the leader of
Qumran (the Teacher of Righteousness), nor do we claim that Jesus' group can be identified in any way with the Qumran community. Still it is only natural for problems like the following to occur to
the minds of people privileged to read the Dead Sea Scrolls now in
translation: Did Jesus, at the time of which we are speaking, have
direct contact of any kind with the Qumran community in the wilderness of Judea? On the supposition that Jesus did have some
personal contact with the Essenes, why does the Bible avoid any
mention of it?

In any event, did Jesus by going to the desert find there anything to slake the dryness of heart and assuage the starvation of
spirit which were with him at Nazareth? Sometime in February of
the year 28 he was baptized by John in the River Jordan, as the
Gospels say. The baptism practiced by the people attached to John
was no mere external rite of initiation into a community as the
baptism practiced at Qumran was. John's baptism was an act of
penitence, symbolizing purification of soul, in accord with the words
in the Old Testament Book of Ezekiel: "I will sprinkle clean water

upon you, and you shall be clean from all your uncleanness, and from all your idols."

Jesus, after being baptized, continued for a time to live with the group, as many others were doing.

Never once did John the prophet ever claim that he himself was the Savior, the Messiah, whom some people took him to be. "I am not the Messiah," he always maintained. "In the words of the prophet Isaiah, 'I am a voice crying aloud in the wilderness, make straight the way of the Lord.' . . . But among you, though you do not know him, stands the one who is to come after me. I am not good enough to unfasten his shoes" (John 1:23-27). All through Old Testament times people had clung to the legend that before the Messiah was to appear, first would come a precursor. John beyond doubt had chosen the role of precursor.

Jesus for the rest of his life retained a feeling of affectionate respect for the fiery prophet dressed in animal skin. Renan's *Vie de Jesus* is a book that is now passe, but Renan was correct where he says that "Jesus, in spite of his own profound originality, submitted to instruction from John, at least for several weeks." As long as Jesus remained with the group, he hardly asserted himself, unobtrusively content to be in the prophet's shadow. Jesus afterward used certain turns of expression taken verbatim from the usage of John, as we see by comparing Matthew 3:7 with 12:34 and again with 23:33. Something like this might be enough to explain why certain disciples of John, after Jesus became active in his own ministry, seemed to consider the new movement to be nothing but a spin-off from theirs. Aware of how Jesus had been their master's favorite disciple, for a long time they considered him one of their own. Eventually this attitude led to a certain discord between themselves and the group that formed around Jesus.

As long as Jesus remained with the group around John the Baptist, he scarcely attracted much attention. Yet his being unassertive was not necessarily the same as agreeing to every aspect of John's community. In my own opinion the shadow of sadness in his eyes did not clear away during the time he spent in docile fellowship with John's disciples.

Jesus, however, was in total sympathy with the voice of John the Baptist when it castigated the Jewish religious establishment—

the Sadducees and the Pharisees in the holy city of Jerusalem, who had control of the temple and the Sanhedrin. The Sadducees, who sprang from the priestly aristocracy, were exploiting to the full the privileges accruing to their administering the temple, and they had lost all rapport with the common people simply by their dogged way of clinging to these hereditary religious functions. They barely managed to retain their position of privilege by their having arranged a working compromise with the Roman governor of Judea.

The Pharisees, in contrast, were in far closer rapport with the common people, yet they had a tendency to absorb themselves in often fruitless casuistry regarding the Law of Torah.

It is no wonder that the voice of John the Baptist denouncing the Jewish establishment was enough to draw the sympathy of Jesus, growing up as he had in Galilee. But the image of God that John embraced was a father-image—the image of wrath, and judgment, and punishment. It was the image of a grim, censorious deity, as he does appear under various circumstances in the Old Testament—a deity destroying whole cities for not submitting to him, or falling into a terrible rage at the sins of his own people, like a despotic father, punishing without mercy the perfidy of all human beings. John the Baptist, wearing camel's skin fastened at the waist with a leather strap, gave notice in advance concerning the wrath of this stern father-image of God: "You brood of vipers! Who warned you to flee from the wrath to come? Bear fruits that befit repentance." Such was God in the Old Testament, raging and punishing, against the backdrop of doomsday and the final judgment.

Is this the true image of God? Maybe Jesus asked himself this very question while staying with the group around John the Baptist. He had known first-hand the lives of ordinary folk in the poverty and squalor of his little town of Nazareth. He had known the stinking sweat of earning his daily bread. He understood well the inevitable frailty of human beings caught in the grind of life. He had witnessed the woes of the sick and the lame. He had some intuition that what these downtrodden people needed, in contrast to the priests and to the doctors of the Law, was something more heartening than a God of wrath, of judgment, and of punishment.

Most likely his image of God had not yet attained sharp focus even within his own heart. But at nighttime in the wilderness of

Judea, as he gazed on the twinkling stars, he could feel the idea welling up from the depths of his spirit. An image of God which differed from the image cherished by John.

> Blessed are the poor in spirit,
>   for theirs is the kingdom of heaven.
> Blessed are they that mourn,
>   for they shall be comforted.

His heart was like a maternal womb to engender an image of God which more closely resembles a gentle mother, the image of God which he would disclose to the people on a mountain by the Lake of Galilee at a later time.

For the moment, Jesus said nothing about it. Keeping his own counsel, he followed the way of John's community and entered upon a retreat of forty days devoted to prayer and fasting in the hills close by the River Jordan. Here belongs the New Testament story of how Jesus turned away the devil's temptations. "Thereupon the Spirit sent him away into the wilderness, and there he remained for forty days tempted by Satan. . . ." (Mark 1:12-13).

Today there is a limestone-like elevation called *Mont de la Quarantaine*, which oral tradition identifies as the place of the temptation. In the words of Henri Daniel-Rops, "The Judean desert is one of the most desolate of places, where eagles soar and jackals howl. A place bereft of any feel for human life, barren landscape with nothing in it to delight the heart."

Anyone visiting the locale will quickly identify the spot. It lies not far from the excavated Qumran monastery of the Essenes. The visitor will readily agree with the words of Father Jean Daniélou: "Matthew writes that Jesus was led by the Spirit to the desert to be tempted there. Yet we have seen that the desert . . . would appear to designate the solitude of the Essenes in the setting in which we find ourselves. Moreover, the traditional locus of the temptation is on the very cliff, slightly north of Qumran, where the scrolls have been discovered."

If Daniélou's hypothesis is correct, we can find the place in the wilderness where Jesus carried on his private retreat nowhere else but in the Qumran monastery of the Essenes. Then we can speculate further that the biblical story of Jesus' being tempted by the devil was composed from the kernel of some event which occurred inside the Qumran monastery.

To repeat, the biblical authors of course do not mention even the existence of the Essene sect or the Qumran community. One reason might be that the authors of the Gospels prudently chose to omit the whole matter because this same Qumran monastery during the Jewish War, which broke out subsequently to the death of Jesus, had been used as a hiding place by the anti-Roman activists belonging to the Zealot party.

The Qumran community connected with the Essenic movement was (again to repeat) a secret society which had been banished from the holy city of Jerusalem and expelled from the mainstream of Jewish religion. The Essene votaries who pursued their way of life in this monastery looked on the establishment back in Jerusalem as men who had surrendered the essential nature of Judaism by their compromise with Rome. The votaries of Qumran were content to lie low, for the time being, yet all their dreams were of the day when under God's protection they would return to Jerusalem and there bring about the restoration of true Judaism. They had developed highly emotional messianic hopes of their own.

The Dead Sea Scrolls, discovered in 1947, include two manuscripts known as *The War Scroll* and *The Scroll of the War of the Sons of Light Against the Sons of Darkness*, both of which reveal how the sect was longing for the day to come when by force of arms they would win their right to leadership and then would wait for the world to submit en masse to the Jewish nation. The inmates of Qumran were pacifist in their personal lives, yet to the very end they aspired to the reality of an earthly "kingdom of God."

To base our judgment on what is written in the Dead Sea Scrolls, the Essenes were in fundamental opposition to the way of thinking in Jesus. First of all, the messianic savior of the Qumran sect was to be an earthly leader; second, they had no thought about saving sinners, nothing to match the thought of Jesus; and third, the Scrolls do speak of brotherly love toward other members of the sect but they say not a word about love toward anyone beyond their tight-knit group, in contrast to this one point which Jesus never ceased to inculcate.

Obviously there do exist a few superficial coincidences between the thought processes of the votaries in the Qumran monastery and the members of the later primitive Christian Church. But what is indicated by their disagreement on this one basic issue?

My own thinking goes like this: While Jesus did his spiritual exercises in solitude not far from the Qumran monastery, the monks pressed him to an ideological showdown. It might even be that the votaries of Qumran tried to recruit him for one of their own. Perhaps this youth with the aching glow in his eye drew personal attention from the religious superior and his assistants at the monastery.

If we follow the story in the Bible, the temptation that the devil presented to Jesus in the wilderness comes down to this: Pursue earthly salvation for the people, and in return I promise to give you the fullness of power on earth—all of which, couched in other words, was precisely what the Essenes in the Qumran monastery were pursuing for their own future.

The spiritual antagonism between Jesus and the Qumran community began from that moment. The picture of Jesus shaking his head to deny the blandishments of the Qumran community comes out dramatically in the biblical scene of Jesus being tempted by the devil. The leaders of the monastery urged him: "If you are the son of God. . . . " This passage shows their genuine feeling about how an earthly kingdom ("bread") was far more practical than talk about any other kind of salvation ("stone"). And then for the first time they unveiled to Jesus their ultimate concern, saying: "All this dominion will I give to you, and the glory that goes with it." Such was the dream they dreamed in Qumran, a dream of the power and the glory to be theirs when they would someday wrest control of the temple in Jerusalem from the Pharisees and the Sadducees. Such were the blandishments to which Jesus promptly shook his head in firm refusal. He found himself incapable of falling in with their way of thinking.

So much for the first painful testing of Jesus. But thanks to the ordeal, he came to discover little by little what it was that he was seeking, and to become accordingly more aware of his own identity. In shaking his head to their inducements, he came to recognize the way which he himself would have to follow.

So ended the forty days of prayer and fasting. When he left the Qumran monastery to return to the bank of the Jordan River and to his association with John the Baptist, the external appearance of Jesus gave little sign of any change, but within himself he had undergone a definitive change.

He had learned what was wanting to the wilderness of Judea and to the men who resorted there—the wilderness of Judea, the brown wasteland of no living creatures save here and there a scanty shrub or thornbush; the barren hills like so many rusty human skulls on the horizon line; the stagnant face of the Dead Sea. What the wilderness failed to give to the men who dwelt there was tenderheartedness. What was wanting to the desert was love. The Qumran group and John's group both preached repentance and the wrath of God. They said nothing concerning love. In gazing at the macabre Dead Sea and the wilderness of Judea, Jesus no doubt recalled the loveliness of springtime back in Galilee. No doubt he also recalled the wretched conditions of life for the people whom he knew there. Does God exist, he asked himself, only to be angry with and to punish lives like theirs? Is it not the very nature of God to pour out his love on these pitiable people? The inhospitable Dead Sea and the barren mountains provided for the Qumran group and for John's group nothing but the image of an outraged deity for them to fear. But Jesus took the opposite view, laying claim to an image of the God of love who comes himself to experience the sorrows of humankind.

Jesus spoke yet to no one about his thinking. A text in the Gospel of John, more than any text in the Synoptic Gospels, clearly shows why, saying that "Jesus for his part would not trust himself to them"—not even to the Baptist's followers (John 2:34).

3 PERILOUS BEGINNINGS

BACK in Jerusalem the Judaic establishment had good reason not to close its eyes to the extraordinary goings-on in the wilderness of Judea. When the Sadducees and Pharisees, priests and scribes, beheld John's baptismal movement drawing the hearts of the people, they were almost panicky in coming to realize that its momentum could no longer be ignored. What they feared more than anything was the threat of an ugly anti-Roman rebellion breaking out in Judea. If any seditious rioting should occur, Pilate, the governor of Judea, would immediately suppress it, but at the same time, in fixing responsibility, he might very well revoke for them those rights invested in the Jewish Sanhedrin, which Rome had recognized exclusively in favor of the Pharisees and the Sadducees. This more than anything else is precisely what alarmed them.

Their fears were not unreasonable. Anti-Roman sentiment was identical with the Jewish spirit of independence, and for the crowds who gathered around John the Baptist the sentiment came also to an easy blend with their religious fervor. I shall be treating this point

later on, but there were among those who joined the group around
John a certain number of hotheads from the Zealot party, which
had its origin in the womb of Galilee, and should any mismanage-
ment occur, there was always the danger of this baptist movement's
developing into a people's rebellion against Rome. (There are certain biblical scholars who interpret John's sect as a quasi-military
organization to carry on the struggle against Rome, but my own
thinking cannot go that far.)

The establishment lost no time in putting together a committee
which they commissioned to investigate John. For the moment,
John was pursuing his ministry at Bethany on the far side of the
Jordan, and that is where the investigators met up with him. Their
line of questioning sought to uncover whether John the Baptist was
not misrepresenting himself. If John were presenting himself as the
Messiah, they would quickly call for a special meeting of the
Sanhedrin and take him to task.

In the face of this inquisition the Baptist adroitly insisted that he
himself was not the Messiah. The gist of their questioning is recorded in John's Gospel, where the investigators ask him bluntly by
whose authority he baptized people and what it was that qualified
him for such an office. But John never ceased to say of himself that
he was only a precursor to the Messiah, and so in the end he
avoided serious trouble.

The investigative team's report to their home base included the
name of Jesus for the information of the high priest presiding in
Jerusalem. Jesus by then had drawn the attention of all in the group
around John, since he obviously was the Baptist's favorite disciple.
From that time on, therefore, the Sadducees and the Sanhedrin
broadened the alert to include keeping a watchful eye on the
movements of Jesus.

Meanwhile, the crowds around John the Baptist included a
certain number of Galileans from the same district as Jesus. These
men were stalwart believers in Judaism, and resolute to the extreme
of being mulish. Being ever conscious of their own ethnic identity,
their political thought was permeated with hatred of Rome. Some of
these Galileans were even affiliated with the Zealot party, which (as
mentioned above) was an organization of radical extremists in the
nationalist resistance of the Jews against Rome. Galilee for several

generations had been notable for its frequent anti-Roman distur-
bances, and following the death of King Herod the Great, the Galileans had planned a revolt against Sabinus, at that time the governor of Judea. Again, in 6 A.D. a Galilean by the name of Judas
had organized a terrorist band which sparked a rebellion against the
Roman legate of Syria when the legate was sent to make an official
survey of resources in Judea. The name "Zealots" refers to the
party which traced its origin to this resistance movement led by
Judas the Galilean.

The men from Galilee (including the Zealots among them) who
associated themselves with the Baptist's group were also looking
earnestly for a leader who hailed from their own part of the country.
It was a natural step for them to turn their attention to Jesus after his
return from fasting in the wilderness.

The Gospel of John relates the charming story of how two of
those Galileans at the River Jordan in the wilderness of Judea made
a direct approach to Jesus and chose him for their teacher.

> The next day John [the Baptist] was standing with two of his disciples
> when Jesus passed by. John looked toward him and said, "There is the
> Lamb of God." The two disciples heard him say this, and followed
> Jesus. When he turned and saw them following him, he asked, "What
> are you looking for?" . . . They went and saw where he was staying and
> spent the rest of the day with him. . . . [And seeking out another
> Galilean] they said to him, "We have found the Messiah" (which is the
> Hebrew for "Christ").

It is an engaging account of how Jesus happened to acquire his
first disciples, but we cannot take the story at face value, for in the
wording of the text lies concealed a tragic note. The way in which
the disciples failed to estimate Jesus correctly is something I call
tragic.

These first disciples of Jesus were actually seeking a man to
assume the leadership of their anti-Roman movement; and beyond
that, they were looking for someone to reform the Jewish religion
corrupted through compromising with Rome. By crying "We have
found the Messiah," they were projecting onto Jesus their own
limited and partisan dreams, for they understood nothing of the
interior spirit of Jesus. Not only the first of his disciples but also those

who gathered around him later—all shared the same lack of insight. We ought to be mindful of how then and there was planted the seed of the tragedy of Judas, who eventually betrayed Jesus.

It is hard to arrive at any precise accounting of why the mind of Jesus could ignore their misunderstanding when he accepted them as disciples. In his own heart perhaps he accepted their aspirations for what they were, while feeling that by and by he could bring these aspirations into harmony with his own intentions. In other words, Jesus may have recognized a certain positive value in these men despite their lack of understanding.

At any rate, so it was that his fellow-countrymen from Galilee began to form a group around Jesus. So it was that the presence of Jesus became conspicuous within the following of John. As for the investigative team dispatched from Jerusalem—naturally, nothing escaped its notice.

The time had come for Jesus and his band of fellow-Galileans to depart from the wilderness of Judea. By then he was fully aware of what was wanting to the men of the wilderness, among the followers of John the Baptist as well as men like the Essenes. Taking shape within himself was an image of God which differed from theirs. Jesus also came to see that it would not be prudent to remain for long in a place where the Jewish leaders were beginning to keep a wary eye on him. He and his first disciples departed the wilderness of Judea by retracing their steps along the road going up the Jordan River, north for some ninety kilometers, to a point from which they veered to the left and returned to their home district in Galilee.

Except for the Gospel of John, the Bible has precious little to report about the movements of Jesus during the early part of his ministry, a period that extends to the time when John the Baptist was thrown into prison. There are also some discrepancies in the chronology of his activities—for example, the famous case of the uproar caused in the temple precincts when Jesus drove out the hucksters, an incident which John's Gospel assigns to the very earliest period of Jesus' ministry, whereas the earlier written Gospel of Mark records the same event as occurring just shortly before his death.

On getting back to Galilee Jesus did not proceed directly to his town of Nazareth, but he returned to his mother's home only after spending time near the Lake of Galilee to gather more disciples. Nothing in the Bible indicates how he was received by all those relatives of his who had been so disgruntled when he first took off for the wilderness of Judea. The well-known story of the prodigal son in the Gospel of Luke might well reflect by analogy something of the state of affairs when his cousins, like the prodigal's elder brother, did not throw off their resentment of Jesus even after he returned—in contrast to the attitude of his mother Mary, who "ran and threw her arms around his neck and kissed him affectionately" (Luke 15:20). I gather this sort of impression from his attending the wedding of an acquaintance at Cana in the company of his mother, and even more from the fact that he moved from Nazareth, taking his mother along, and established a home with her in Capernaum on the Lake of Galilee (John 2:12; Matthew 4:13).

The wedding at Cana, reported in John's Gospel, is a cheerful story coming like a springtime zephyr between other events in the Bible more apt to be somewhat depressing. Among the disciples whom Jesus recruited from John the Baptist's following was a man from Cana by the name of Nathanael, and it is possible that the wedding party was for one of Nathanael's kinfolk.

By oral tradition Cana is identified with a homely little town existing today about ten kilometers from Nazareth. The town is surrounded by low-lying reddish-brown hills with olive orchards, and if we walk in the little streets through the deep shade cast by the trees even in broad daylight, we hear the chickens clucking from the houses along both sides of the street. It was most likely springtime when Jesus came here for the wedding, when flowers were abloom in the fields and in the groves. The villagers all enjoyed the wine, tumbling over themselves in high hilarity, and Jesus, too, broke out in audible laughter with one cup on another. In Luke 7:34 his enemies say about Jesus behind his back, "Look at him—a glutton and a drinker." Yet even if we concede that such mudslinging cannot be taken literally—according to Stauffer's findings, the Jews of the time pinned these epithets on any disaffected person—still it is clear from the story of Cana that in mixing socially with others, Jesus by no means wore only a grumpy face.

It is not by accident that the Gospel of John weaves into the

very earliest period of Jesus' public life this human-interest story of
the wedding that comes across with the lilt of springtime. The intention is to depict a contrast with the winter of his austerities in the
forbidding wilderness of Judea. The story shows in bold relief how
Jesus had survived the shortcomings of the wilderness and how he
had moved beyond the ill-humored image of God upheld by the
sectarians there. Jesus thoroughly enjoyed the wedding party of the
young lovers. It is worth our while to compare his laughing face
putting away the drinks, with the face of John the Baptist, the man
clothed in animal hide fastened at the waist with a leather strap,
haranguing people forever about the wrath of God. This story discovers to us the beaming *joie de vivre* of Jesus, who had moved
beyond the wilderness and beyond the religious brotherhood of
John. Hunter hits the mark where he says: "In what does the
prophetic message of Jesus differ from John's? The preaching of
John was a burden heavy with the old-time threat of utter destruc-
tion. But the preaching of Jesus is a song of joy." To paraphrase a
certain verse in Mark, the face of John the Baptist's disciples per-
sonified sobriety itself, whereas the disciples of Jesus were like
guests at a wedding party (Mark 2:18).

There is still another reason why John's Gospel records the
marriage at Cana as being an event of the opening phase. The
reason lies in the symbolic action of Jesus' "changing water into
wine" while seated at the wedding. This action of Jesus, described
in the Gospel as a miracle, in fact gives us an insight into the relationship of Jesus with the disciples. The disciples, drawn from the
followers of John, continued to believe that Jesus would restore the
lost purity of the Jewish religion and that he would serve as their
leader in the struggle against Roman oppression; but on the part of
Jesus, this scene at the wedding suggests that what he had in mind
was, eventually and only gradually, to raise the disciples' very
human dream (the "water") in the sublime level of his own world
(the "wine").

After the sojourn at Cana, Jesus moved his residence from
Nazareth to Capernaum. Although nothing is said in the other Gospels, John's Gospel records that shortly after this move, Jesus paid a
brief visit to Judea and Jerusalem. According to the record it appears that he followed the method of John the Baptist's followers by

administering the rite of baptism. The fact is, however, that this procedure was not so much the idea of Jesus himself; his disciples were only continuing the ordinary practice of John the Baptist's group. Jesus still lent support to John the Baptist by maintaining his usual unassuming posture, being not yet prepared to reveal to the public his own special character.

Then it happened. Without warning, King Herod Antipas struck a blow to imprison John the Baptist. According to the Bible (Luke 3:19ff.), John was arrested because he had openly denounced the king for entering an incestuous marriage with Herodias, the wife of his own half brother, Herod Philip II (4 B.C.- 34 A.D.). The couple had become acquainted while Herod Antipas was staying for a while in Rome. Since Herodias herself was the daughter of still another brother of Herod Antipas, the two were, legally speaking, related to each other also as uncle and niece. Furthermore, being already married to a daughter of Aretas IV, the Arabian king of the Nabateans, Antipas discarded this lawful wife and then stepped out of bounds into the new union. Nevertheless, beyond the point made in John the Baptist's denunciation, Herod Antipas secretly possessed a still more deep-seated problem. The censure coming from John really did no more than give to the king an open pretext for imprisoning him. Flavius Josephus, the historian of the period, has defined with clarity the issue that really bothered King Herod Antipas:

> Herod feared that John's influence with the common people might lead them to rebellion. It was thought that the people would follow John in any move whatsoever if John were only to recommend it. The king considered it the better part of prudence to wipe out John before the fact, rather than passively to await the rebellion which John might stir up, and then to be left with nothing but regrets for permitting himself to become so entangled in troubles. Thanks to this anxiety of Herod, John was incarcerated in the fortress of Machaerus, and there he was put to death (*Antiquities of the Jews*).

Of course the Baptist himself never had any idea of rebelling with force of arms. But whatever the leader's thought might be, situations do occur where the common people, having once established their leader, are then swept away in some other direction with

the force of an avalanche. Just as Jesus was misunderstood by his
disciples to be an anti-Roman nationalist leader, so it is not strange
to imagine that many of the common people might take a similar
view of John the Baptist. The time also happened to be at the very
moment, the year 30 of the Christian era, when Sejanus, court
favorite of the Emperor Tiberius, took steps toward his own overall
Roman solution to the Jewish problem. Pilate, the governor of
Judea, enjoyed the support of Sejanus. And King Herod Antipas
was justifiably sensitive to the state of affairs. Being himself deferen-
tial to Rome, he was for that reason forever cautious about his
relation to Pilate, hoping to be free of the slightest suspicion regarding his fealty. It was therefore natural for him to be uneasy about
John the Baptist and his rude Galilean supporters.

Flavius Josephus wrote nothing in so many words about who it
was who profited most from the plight of Herod Antipas and from
his temperament—I refer to the religious leadership in Jerusalem.
The religious establishment had been unable to hale John into court
on any legality, based on the reports submitted by the investigative
team previously sent out to question the prophet, yet it is permissi-
ble to think that the Sanhedrin actually attained its own ends
through the action taken by Herod. The concern of both parties for
self-preservation explains this converging of aims between the
Sanhedrin and Herod Antipas.

It is not to be thought that the perilous fate of John the Baptist
did not generate waves which were to affect his favorite disciple
Jesus. This could explain why the Gospels have almost nothing to
say concerning the progress of Jesus during his early ministry. The
unsettling background may also have some connection with how
Jesus, after moving with his mother to a new home in Capernaum
on the Lake of Galilee, proceeded from there to keep changing his
own whereabouts from place to place within the northern reaches of
Judea.

Where did Jesus hear about John being arrested? According to
Stauffer it was in Jerusalem, where he had gone to worship in the
temple and to celebrate the feast of Booths in the autumn of the
year 30. The feast of Booths was a week-long festival to
memorialize the nomadic desert life of the forefathers and to celebrate the autumn harvest.

Stauffer's ideas are forever harebrained but just this once we must not gainsay what he relates of the way in which the priests and the Pharisees and the Sadducees questioned Jesus during his sojourn in Jerusalem, and how Jesus was in danger of his life (John 5:18). The priests in the establishment were already furnished with disturbing memories concerning Jesus, based on the reports of their own investigation team.

On the Sabbath day of rest during the festival, Jesus in the company of his disciples was caring for the sick people who congregated at the Pool of Bethesda, close by the Sheep Gate in the city walls of Jerusalem. The blind and the paralytic and the lame assembled there because of an old wives' tale that a cure awaited the first one to enter the water after ripples were stirred on the pool by the intermittent inflow. For the priests, and especially for the Pharisees with them, it was considered nothing less than sacrilegious for anyone to nurse the sick in disregard of the Sabbath, the day on which all manner of work was prohibited by the Law of Torah. On this pretext they moved to set the scene for haling Jesus into court. They planned to grab the golden opportunity of John the Baptist's arrest to take his favorite disciple also into custody. A passage in the third chapter of John's Gospel (verses 17-47) reflects the pattern of their questions and the answers of Jesus on this occasion. But they did not succeed in digging up anything definite to charge him with, and the priests in the seats of power could do nothing except to let him go free.

John the Baptist was not so fortunate. He had been caught in the snare set by Herod Antipas when he was baptizing at Aennon in the vicinity of Salim. He was arrested and then imprisoned inside the stronghold of Machaerus, on the limits of the king's domain. In all the visits I have made to various biblical sites, unfortunately I was never able to get to Machaerus, but Daniel-Rops gives this description of the place:

Machaerus today is a heap of ruins on the plateau of Moab, which stretches out to the East toward the Arabian Desert but which, on the West, falls steeply into the vertiginous gorge of the Dead Sea. There was formerly a town here with a considerable caravan traffic, but nothing of it remains except a causeway of broken stones, the debris of houses, and the foundations of a Temple of the Sun. Yet on the sharp cone of the adjoining hill can still be seen vestiges of the fortress where the Forerunner ended his days. . . . The foundations of the surrounding wall are still visible and in the center there is a deep well, a cistern and two turrets, in one of which can still be seen the holes in the masonry for the rings of the prisoners' chains.

The end of John the Baptist deeply saddened Jesus, and it certainly carried its own suggestion about how he himself should proceed from that time on. In this turn of events Jesus learned how it can happen that after a leader takes the masses into tow, the masses might then overwhelm the leader and move in a direction opposed to their leader's intent. From this time on, a certain prudential concern appears in the demeanor of Jesus dealing with his disciples, one consideration most likely being that he himself was not of a mind to meet a fate like that of John the Baptist.

After the dangerous sojourn in Jerusalem for the feast of Booths, Jesus decided to return to Galilee by passing straight through Samaria, avoiding the familiar route which led from Jerusalem via Jericho and then along the River Jordan. I can think of two reasons: for one thing, it is true that the Samaritans nurtured hard feelings against the Jews, and the feelings were returned in kind by the Jews, who considered them perverted believers and hence despised them even more than they did the pagans. The Jews in fact had a saying that "the water in Samaria is dirtier than pig slops." Still, Jesus may have thought that Samaria was safer for him and his party than the other possibility of their being hounded as friends of John the Baptist.

There is another reason. What prompted Jesus to go home by way of Samaria was something more than seeking to avoid late summer heat in the valley and more than mere thought for his personal safety. It was rather what Jesus did all his life—by choosing this route he wished to demonstrate to his disciples the pre-eminent charity which drew him in predilection to the loathsome ones of the world, to the souls despised and rejected by others. This journey was one aspect of his characteristic opposition to those men of power in Jerusalem who were sticklers for Sabbath observance and similar points of the Law but were unmindful of charity.

The road through Samaria, from Bethel to Engannin by way of

Shechem, was a route to be avoided by Jews of that time for the simple reason that the Samaritans in return really hated the Jews and were not always devoid of any thought for retaliation.

But the Gospel parable of the Good Samaritan (Luke 10:13ff.) and the story of the Samaritan leper both demonstrate how Jesus himself bore not a trace of the old Jewish feeling.

After walking fifty kilometers, he and the disciples arrived about noon in the town of Shechem. To this day Shechem is a rather isolated town, where the only thing to look at is a head-on view of desolate Mount Gerizim. While the disciples were off in search of food, Jesus spoke with a woman, from whom he had begged a drink of water.

"Take my word for it, madam," Jesus said. "[You worship on Mount Gerizim here.] A time is coming when you will worship the Father neither on this mountain nor in Jerusalem."

Obviously these words are equivalent to a declaration considered blasphemous by those who held power in the sacred temple of Jerusalem. Yet these words constitute the first proclamation from Jesus that we have something more sacred than even the temple, something more sublime, something more profound—we have the God of love.

What draws our interest here is that Jesus takes advantage of the absence of his own disciples to confide in this Samaritan woman despised by the Jews, and a woman trapped in her own life of poverty and shame. His words were not for the ears of the disciples. He realized the depth of the chasm, yet to be spanned, between himself and them. He spoke his true mind to this Samaritan woman detested by the Jews, and not to his disciples.

He tarried in Samaritan country for two days. But during that time was Jesus aware perhaps of how the day would come when the Samaritans, whom he treated so amiably, would turn their backs and refuse him lodging for the night?

Be that as it may, except for the scanty record in John's Gospel regarding this early period, the other Gospels say hardly anything about it. The reason? The evangelists, at the time they were writing (as I imagine it), were much concerned about relations between the infant Christian Church and the Roman world. The Gospel of Mark, the earliest Gospel in the Bible as we have it, is said to have been composed sometime between the years 65 and 75, shortly after Rome with a mighty effort had suppressed a four-year-long rebellion by the Jews, when Roman resentment against the Jews was most intense. It could very well be that Mark the evangelist, as far as possible, chose to omit from his life of Jesus any doings related to the nationalist movement, and especially any Christian connection with the party of the Zealots, which had generated the Jewish revolt—all with a mind to forestall any move by Rome to suppress the infant Church. The same considerations may have been reason for all the evangelists to play down the movement of John the Baptist and to omit entirely any mention of the Essenes.

But in our own day we cannot afford to ignore the background of the early career of Jesus which relates him to the activities of John the Baptist and to the movement of the ultra-nationalists. The more the evangelists tend to be vague about it, the more the present-day reader can sense the importance of this background.

John the Baptist's deplorable death left a deep scar in the heart of Jesus. From then on, the disciples saw Jesus himself as a second John the Baptist. The look in their eyes was the same as it had been for John. John the Baptist's tragic end brought a sense of victory to the religious leaders in Jerusalem, but only for a moment, because the chronic sentiments of the common people, including the Galileans, remained in force like burning coals.

4 SPRINGTIME IN GALILEE

At this time I would like to interrupt for a moment the chronological order in my narrative to say a few words about the point of view I take in writing this life of Jesus.

People generally recognize that the New Testament, as we have it, does not always stay with the "real facts" in depicting the career of Jesus. Protestants and Catholics alike concede this point. For example, in reading and comparing the Synoptic Gospels of Matthew, Mark, and Luke, side by side with the Gospel of John, we can expect to find identical accounts of the doings of Jesus presented in different chronological orders. (I have already called attention, for example, to how the Synoptics place the incident of Jesus' cleansing the temple of Jerusalem at a time only shortly before his death, whereas John places the same event in the earliest period of the public life.) Various scholars propose various theories to cover such discrepancies, but no one theory is incontrovertible. The question of how to arrange these discrepant elements into a single life of Jesus will therefore be determined on the basis of that image of

Jesus grasped by the person who reads the Bible.

After the research done by the German biblical scholar Rudolph Bultmann, we know that woven into the New Testament are certain passages which originated in the *kerygma* (confession of faith) of the primitive Christian Church. We also know that after the death of Jesus the authors of the Bible composed their various lives of Jesus, each in his own peculiar style, after they had gathered eye-witness accounts concerning Jesus, along with local traditions and folk stories from different parts of the country, many of which they incorporated into their own compositions along with the genuine and readily available historical source known as the sayings of Jesus. Consequently the various lives of Jesus in the Bible, while they certainly portray consistent *truth*, on various points of particular *fact* were not necessarily written in the modern spirit of accurate reporting. Many scholars point out that passages presented in the Bible as being the precise words of Jesus himself in fact represent the kerygma of the primitive Christian Church; again there are scholars who say that certain actions of Jesus, presented as really happening in a certain town or village, are in fact simply legends handed down in that particular town or village. In his process of trying to sort out fact from fiction, Bultmann winds up with the hopeless declaration that "the image of the historical Jesus in the Bible becomes ever more elusive for us."

From such a point of view, is there any possibility left for us to write an accurate life of Jesus? Anyone who feels that indeed it is impossible to write a factual life of Jesus, based only on the materials presently available, is perhaps right in line with the feeling of these biblical scholars.

Further consideration, however, will cause us to ask if it is possible to produce an accurate biography of anybody at all, whether the subject be Jesus or any other person. The biographer proceeds to collect as much material as he can about the life of some particular person, but his material for the most part will consist of impressions of the subject's personality as observed by others; and since these personal impressions depend on varying particular points of view, the biographer when all is said and done can hope to close in on his subject only by using, as it were, the eyeglasses belonging to third parties. The case of Jesus is the same. Obviously we cannot retrace the life of Jesus *with absolute precision*. We cannot even set down the doings of Jesus exactly in the order in which they occurred. Why is it, nevertheless, that when we read the Bible, we do feel that we are getting from the text a lively image of Jesus himself and the people around him? It is because the image of Jesus in the Bible is a true portrait, even if it is not the Jesus of detailed fact.

It was a brief period of only two years, yet during these two years the status of Jesus changed remarkably. In the turning of events occasioned by the imprisonment of John the Baptist, this man who had been an obscure carpenter in the town of Nazareth abruptly became an object of widespread attention from the Jews among whom he moved, their attention being of two kinds—one of high hope, the other of suspicion.

In the first instance, the eyes of high expectation were the eyes of his disciples and of the lower class people in Galilee who had centered their warmhearted favor on John the Baptist. Some of them thought Jesus was the successor to John the Baptist, and many again fixed on Jesus the wild dream that besides merely reforming the Jewish religion, he might also become their leader who would drive the Gentiles from the occupied land of Judah. There is evidence for this in the words used by one of the disciples to express his grief after the death of Jesus: "But we had been hoping that he was the man to liberate Israel."

In the second instance, the eyes of suspicion were those of the Sadducees and the Pharisees in control of the temple in Jerusalem, and the eyes of the Sanhedrin. They came to see Jesus as a threat, a man who might gradually prove to be their undoing. Jesus came through to them as an insidious self-appointed reformer of Jewish religion, as an agitator who could eventually rouse the masses.

Jesus himself was painfully aware of these two sets of eyes. He took to heart the hateful looks he drew from certain Jewish leaders, and the misapprehending looks that came from the disciples and from the Galileans who crowded around him. Neither side appreciated his true purpose. No one had eyes to see that his true intent was aimed at one end only—to bear witness to the love of God.

> Blessed are the poor in spirit,
>   for theirs is the kingdom of heaven.
> Blessed are those who mourn,
>   for they shall be comforted.

In these words of his, like twinkling stars, glows an image of the God of love. And yet, to judge from his experience while living in the town of Nazareth, the poor in fact remained in their misery, and those who wept were not in fact consoled. The stars on which he gazed in the wilderness of Judea were cold as ice; the Dead Sea, in which no living creature stirred, and the mountains behind the sea, revealed no more than a God who is prone to anger and who punishes and who sits in judgment. This extremely severe father-image of God had prevailed throughout the Old Testament. John the Baptist and his group inherited that image, and Jesus in their company quickly perceived what was wanting to them.

Merely talking about "the love of God" and "the God of love" is easy, although human beings trapped in life's cruel realities feel nothing but God's cold-hearted silence rather than God's love. To judge from life's cruel realities it is easier to think about a God of wrath and retribution than to believe in the God of love. Consequently, even if the Old Testament did on occasion speak of the love of God, the image of God that prevailed in people's hearts was one of fear. How can people grasp the love of God when those who obviously are poor in spirit and those who mourn are in fact without redress of any kind?

Jesus was, of course, aware of the incongruity. Faith in the love of God was ablaze in his own heart, yet his faith was not the same as ignoring contradictions—not in the least, for the overriding theme that ran through his life was his concern for how he might demonstrate the existence of the God of love and make it possible for other people to know the love of God. This is the theme which from this point on will drive us forward in discoursing of the life of Jesus. In what way did Jesus strive to demonstrate the love of God, so difficult of belief in the eyes of people living in the material world? That very question provides the warp on which we shall weave the various threads in our life of Jesus.

"After John had been arrested, Jesus came into Galilee proclaiming the Gospel of God: 'The time has come; the kingdom of God is upon you; repent, and believe in the Gospel.'"

The fourteenth verse of Chapter 1 in the Gospel of Mark thus records the opening move of Jesus in Galilee. The Church calls the life of Jesus, from that point on, the public life of Jesus.

Public life it was, and yet how different is the proclamation made by Jesus from the earlier proclamation of John the Baptist.

John the Baptist cried: "You vipers' brood! Who warned you to escape from the coming retribution? Then prove your repentance by the fruit it bears. . . . Already the axe is laid to the roots of the trees, and every tree that fails to produce good fruit is cut down and thrown on the fire."

What is being proclaimed is the same for both, yet from John the message came as a terrifying threat. It was the cry from the wilderness. For those who failed to produce good fruits in face of the threat, there was the hint of God's judgment, his rage, his vengeance. They would be "cut down and thrown on the fire."

But the proclamation of Jesus is the Gospel. The word "Gospel" by its etymology denotes something joyful. The proclamation from Jesus contained no words of menace to make the hearers tremble, in contrast to the proclamation that came from John. Jesus made no allusion to anything like the wrath of God and his vengeance. Even the exhortation "Repent!"—the same word used by John—can be safely interpreted as meaning something like: "Don't wander away!"

Seeing these two proclamations side by side, we are captivated by the sense of how finally a new light is added to the more obscure vision of the Old Testament world. We get the impression of the long long night being finished, the first streak of dawn breaking through. Or to employ another image, anybody who has traveled to Israel can recall the scenery along the shore of the Lake of Galilee and how it contrasts sharply with the wilderness of Judea.

The shore of the Lake of Galilee was where Jesus made his proclamation. What a tremendous shift from the shore of the Dead Sea and its adjacent wilderness of Judea, which supports not a single tree or a single blade of grass. The inhabitants may have been wretchedly poor, but the landscape was beneficent and altogether beautiful, with gentle hills where flocks of sheep could pasture on the grass, and with groves of lofty eucalyptus trees reflecting their image in the surface of the lake; breezes blowing through the trees; yellow chrysanthemums and red anemones blooming wild in the open fields; and far out on the lake the floating boats of the fishermen. Human society was pathetic, but the natural setting was benign.

Come to me, all whose work is hard, whose load is heavy; and I will give you relief (Matthew 11:28).

Reading these words of Jesus in the Gospel of Matthew, we can picture him with arms extended wide, standing by the shore of the lake. The breeze coming from across the water carries the voice of his summons to all the oppressed and impoverished towns and villages around the lake. Emerging from the dingy interiors of their houses are the old men and women, one after another—the cripples and the blind—all of whom have heard his voice: "Come to me, all whose work is hard, whose load is heavy, and I will give you relief."

Along the lake stood fishing towns like Capernaum and Magdala and Bethsaida. Not directly on the shoreline but nestled in the lofty hills close by the lake were towns like Chorazin. The towns were too small to merit the name of city, and many of the people made their livelihood by harvesting fish from the lake. In our own day most of these ancient towns lie buried underground and their remains cannot, in every case, be identified with any certitude. Magdala lies beneath a grove of eucalyptus standing in a grassy open field that blooms with wild flowers. The site of Capernaum—there are two opinions about its actual location—is nothing but the excavated ruins of a synagogue (erected after the time of Jesus) and of a few old houses that belonged to the ancient inhabitants. And Chorazin up in the hills, the town which never did give Jesus a hearing, now lies in the sleep of death with nothing to show for itself but the rubble of blackened chunks of masonry scattered here and there.

Jesus moved from one to another of these fishing villages. With no more evidence than what the Bible provides, it is worth noting that he avoided setting foot apparently only in Tiberias, the biggest town on the lake, the town built by Herod Antipas.

Small as the villages might be, there was in every one of them a house of Jewish worship called the synagogue. These synagogues were next in importance to the temple of Jerusalem as places for religious Jews to fulfill their obligations of divine worship. Water pots for ritual purification were placed inside, at the entrance to a rectangular area partitioned off by a colonnade, and the walls of the inner hall were decorated with mosaic designs. Because the main entrance of a synagogue was always laid out to face in the direction of Jerusalem, in the time of Jesus the synagogues of Galilee invariably faced toward the south. The synagogues were opened morning and afternoon on the sabbath and on religious feast days; and when the people were assembled, the worship service opened with a prayer called by its initial word the *Shema* ("Hear, O Israel!"), which was followed then by readings aloud from the Torah, and the service eventually came to a close with an Amen from the presiding elder in the assembly.

Jesus used these worship services in the synagogue to speak to the villagers. If the synagogue was closed, he might address whatever people would gather together on a hillside near the lake or in an open field. His most attentive listeners were the fishermen and their families around the lake, and not the priests or the doctors of the Law. By his former life as one of the working class Jesus was intimately acquainted with the people's way of life; his talks were easy to follow, and he usually began by telling some homely story drawn from daily life. His parables never wanted for a sense of realism, enough to draw knowing nods of approval from everyone. The stories were reminiscent of workaday sweat.

During this early period it isn't clear whether Jesus moved about alone or whether he took his disciples with him. The disciples had their own work near the lake, so most likely only when they were free did they go with him to row the boat as he moved from place to place along the shore. At other times, most likely Jesus walked by himself along the country roads ablaze with all the wild flowers of the lake region, to visit the neighboring towns. In contrast to the prophets of old, he did not preach God's wrath and chastisement. He only spoke about the imminent kingdom of God, the God of love. Unlike the priests and the scribes, he never engaged with the fishermen and their families in any hair-splitting discussions concerning the Law, or Torah. He himself was faithful to the precepts of Judaic Law, yet when a practical application of the Law could not be rooted in charity, he was courageous enough to make an exception.

Around the lake, where nature was so beautiful and the lives of the people so wretched, the towns were full of sick and crippled ones neglected by their neighbors and even by their own families. There were others, men and women like the tax collectors and the prostitutes, who were condemned by the priests. Reading the New Testament provides a picture of Jesus with his loving predilection for drawing close to men and women who were otherwise forsaken or held in contempt. In the villages around the lake were victims of malaria, whom healthy people despised for being possessed by an evil spirit, yet Jesus tended their needs. The lepers, forbidden to approach any village or town, were considered under the Law to be unclean and to be the recipients of punishment from God (Leviticus 13:14), yet Jesus ignored that part of the Law and tried to help them. He enlisted into his group of close disciples one of the tax collectors who were always objects of derision. Nor did he turn up his nose at the prostitutes, always the objects of public disdain.

The Gospels have many stories about Jesus and these abandoned souls. The stories are of two kinds: one is where Jesus heals their infirmities by a miracle, what are termed "miracle stories"; the other is where, rather than performing a miracle, Jesus simply shares with them their pitiable suffering—in other words, "consolation stories." Why is it then that, between the two, it is the consolation stories which carry a greater sense of reality than do the miracle stories? Why is it that the consolation stories are far more effective in portraying a lifelike picture of Jesus and in bringing vividly before our eyes the circumstances of the story?

The following narrative, for example, occurs in the seventh chapter of Luke, beginning with verse 36:

One of the Pharisees invited him to a meal with him. He entered the home of the Pharisee and reclined on a couch; and without warning, a woman who was a scandal in the town [a harlot] came in. After making sure that he was at table in the home of the Pharisee, she brought with her an alabaster flask of perfume, took her stand behind him at his feet, and wept. Yielding to an impulse, she rained her tears on his feet and wiped them with her hair.

On reading this passage we can close our eyes and envision the circumstances not explicitly recorded.

Perhaps the harlot in the story was an impoverished girl in Magdala or some such place. She gave herself to any man in order to stay alive, and the man sneeringly gave her money in return for the fun of toying with her while she lay motionless beside him, empty eyes staring open in the dark.

From whom did she hear about Jesus? How did she get the idea of going to him? It could be that she had heard about Jesus one night from a man who had bought her service. It might even be that she caught sight of Jesus from a distance while he was sitting, tired and quiet, by the edge of the lake. She certainly knew very little about the sort of person Jesus was. Only from his demeanor did she gather the inexpressible kindly attitude that was his. Here was a woman, seasoned to her own misery and the contempt of others, who could recognize by instinct the sort of person who has real kindness of heart.

Because the house where Jesus was at table belonged to a Pharisee, when the woman entered, the servants likely tried to prevent her. To the Pharisees she was only a lowly whore to whom they held themselves forbidden to give so much as the time of day. In the world of the Old Testament these females were often the target of vehement denunciation from the prophets. She must have therefore shaken loose from the servants, stepped into the dining room, and walked straight toward Jesus through the gauntlet of open mouthed stares turning on her from everyone at table.

She spoke nothing. In silence she looked intently on Jesus. Soon the tears that formed in her eyes began to overflow. The tears alone bespoke the sorrow she knew. "She rained her tears on his feet " The trenchant expression is enough to have us know how pitiably wretched she was feeling.

The tears told Jesus everything. He understood her being a

public object of contempt through half of her life, eating her heart
out in lonely misery. The tears were enough. God rejoiced to welcome her: Your tears are enough. Don't weep anymore. As for me,
I understand how unhappy you have been.

Jesus responded with gentleness. The words he quietly spoke
are among the most beautiful in all the Bible. "Her sins, which are
many, are forgiven, for she loved much."

Whoever loves much will be forgiven much.

A consolation story like this appeals to us far more vividly than
do many of the miracle stories concerning Jesus. The words chosen
convey the woman's sadness—"She rained her tears on his
feet"—and the gently spoken words of forgiveness—"Whoever
loves much will be forgiven much"—have a ring to them which
never fails to stir our emotions.

I will cite another one of the consolation stories. Matthew,
Mark, and Luke each presents his own account of what happened
with the woman who suffered from chronic bleeding of the uterus.

> There was in the crowd a woman who had a flow of blood for twelve
> years, and who had suffered much under many physicians, and had
> spent all she had, and was not better but rather grew worse. She had
> heard the reports about Jesus, and came up behind him in the crowd and
> touched his garment. . . . Jesus said, "Who touched my garment?"
> (Mark 5:25).

This event too occurred in a town by the Lake of Galilee. The
woman, mingling unobtrusively in the crowd that was pressing in to
get a close look at Jesus, had suffered so long from her incurable
hemorrhaging that her act of touching a trembling finger to his
clothing was like a drowning person's catching at a straw. At merely
the touch of this timid finger Jesus felt all the burden of her suffering
and the desperation which made her grasp at straws.

"Who touched my clothes?" he said, turning to the disciples.
They laughed, replying, "You see the crowd pressing upon you and
yet you ask, 'Who touched me?' How can you avoid being jostled?"

"No, you're wrong," said Jesus, shaking his head. "Somebody
has touched my clothing."

Then among all the faces intently watching him, he distin-
guished the frightened look on one woman's face.

The story leads into the miracle story of how Jesus healed the woman's malady, but to me the affecting part is how Jesus felt all the woman's heartbreaking suffering through the touch of her trembling finger against his clothing—more moving than the sequel in which he cures her ailment with a miracle. The woman's finger reaches furtively from behind other people, and when it barely comes in contact with his outer garment, Jesus turns and understands her suffering. From the single trembling finger we complete the picture of the woman's frightened face and the heart-stricken look from the face of Jesus.

If the consolation stories seem more realistic than do the miracle stories, could the explanation be that the miracles of Jesus were put into writing only after the many oral traditions concerning Jesus had been collected from the back country towns of Galilee, in contrast to the other stories based on eyewitness accounts still fresh in the memory of the disciples themselves and written down with no embroidering?

The disciples must have witnessed many scenes of Jesus coming in contact with unfortunate people in the Galilean towns. The disciples at those times could see the look on the faces of the woman with the uterine hemorrhage and of the lepers and the prostitutes, and they would each time be impressed with how all these misfortunate people fixed their heart-breaking gaze on Jesus. Nor could they ever forget the sympathetic look of Jesus toward the sufferers. The disciples simply then reported their powerful impressions to the evangelists, who in turn were able to represent these same impressions in their written word with no elaborations.

What draws our hearts in the consolation stories is the way they picture Jesus spending his time on these sorrows in the sort of men and women to whom others paid no attention. In the towns of Galilee Jesus would sit so as to be at the level of the lepers and the cripples who came crawling to him from their dismal hovels; nor did he hide his sympathies for people like the harlots and the tax collectors who were openly despised by others. The towns around the lake were small and wretched, but they were the world of Jesus. He felt that one by one the griefs of all the people in the world were coming to rest on his own shoulders. The sorrows began to weigh on his back with an onerous crunch, like the heavy cross that he himself would have to carry sometime in the future. It is the realism in the consolation stories that accounts for our own vivid sense of the kind of person Jesus was.

Yet Jesus even at the time was well aware of something else, namely, love's futility in the world of material values. He loved the unfortunate ones, yet he also understood that once even they came to know love's futility, they too would be turning against him. When all is said and done, the hard fact remains that human beings are on the lookout for practical and tangible results. The sick after all were asking him to be cured, the lame to be able to walk, and the blind for their eyes to be opened—they sought tangible benefits. Yet love is an act which in this visible world bears no direct correlation with tangible benefits. The passion of Jesus begins right here. With a touch of sadness he demurred on one occasion: "Unless you see signs and wonders you will not believe" (John 4:48).

This pain of Jesus hides in the background of every miracle story written into the New Testament. More important than the conventional question of whether Jesus did or did not perform miracles, the fact is that the miracle stories, merely as stories, enable us to appreciate the sad outcome of people's looking to Jesus not for his gift of love but only for signs and wonders. Verse 28 in Chapter 4 of Luke's Gospel happens to reveal how people became infuriated if their hopes were not fulfilled. This particular citation is no more than a single line of print, but it gives an important hint for our reading of the miracle stories.

Still, in the early days of Jesus' ministry the situation was different. Along the shore of the lake, people welcomed him as "the One who was to come." There were several reasons behind this reception.

People had not yet recovered from their shock at John the Baptist's being arrested. John's prophetic voice crying in the wilderness had exerted its pull on many hearts and left them in the hope that John himself was the man who would deliver Israel from Roman oppression. Their hopes collapsed with the prophet's sudden catastrophe. Had God once more retired to his realm of silence? The fervent strict-observing Jews of Galilee had reason to be disheartened and full of regret on hearing the news, for at that very time the imperial government in Rome was moving toward a still more oppressive policy toward the Jews. The new policy was designed by a man named Sejanus, the political mover in the court of the emperor, and in the spring of this same year Sejanus issued an order for Pilate the governor to engrave the Roman emperor's emblem on all the coinage. Sejanus had also rescinded the right of the Sanhedrin to execute sentences of death, and the priests and scribes in Jerusalem were powerless to do anything except submit to these new measures of oppression. No storm of protest had broken out as yet, but the unsettled atmosphere was beginning to stir. People were longing for somebody else to take up the objectives of John the Baptist. At that very moment, Jesus presented himself on the shore of the lake.

At first the number of those who listened to Jesus was likely too small to be noticed, but it didn't take long for the crowds to grow in size.

An analysis reveals that these crowds consisted of the disciples, properly so called, and then all the ordinary people who shared the sentiments of the disciples, then the wretched, poverty-stricken women and children and old folks, and finally the sick.

We don't have reliable statistics on the population around the lake. According to Flavius Josephus, "there were 240 cities and towns in the area with a minimum of 15,000 people in the smallest of the towns," but figures like these are a gross exaggeration, obvious to anyone who ever visited Galilee.

While the inhabitants nursed their dark mood of frustration over the arrest of John the Baptist, the word got around of how Jesus had been the model disciple in John's community, and people quickly began thinking of him as the Baptist's successor (Luke 9:7; Matthew 16:13).

One day became another, and the crowds pressing about the frail-looking figure of Jesus began to overwhelm him. To quote the words of the Bible: "The news spread rapidly, and he was spoken of all over the district of Galilee" (Mark 1:28). "Such a crowd collected in Capernaum that the space in front of the door was not big enough to hold them" (Mark 2:2), and it is even reported that he couldn't find time to eat his meals.

Jesus gradually became the object of all their dreams. Although different people had somewhat different dreams to fasten on him, to the vast majority he seemed to be in the mold of John the Baptist or Elijah or any of the prophets of old, the one man who could become their leader. In the dreams of the ultra-nationalists, he would be the one to eventually drive the Romans out of Palestine, the man who had it in him to restore their pride to the Jews. The Zealots eyed him as a possible leader to fire their armed resistance. Finally, there were the women and the old folks and the sick, who looked upon him as a holy man displaying "deeds of power" and healing their infirmities.

Such were the whirlpools of misconception into which Jesus launched his ministry. Overwhelmed by the crowds on every side, what saddened him most was to be aware of how far the people were misinterpreting his aim. In his own mind he had one objective only—to manifest the God of love who transcends this visible world. For the time being, the only obstacles he had to overcome were the pleas and the looks of wild expectation from the masses of men and women pressing about him. Even while Jesus stood in the circle of his own disciples, he was alone.

5 SPIES

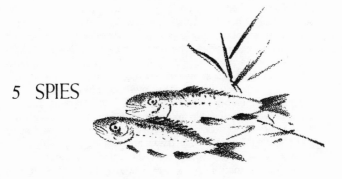

By now the priests and the scribes in control of the temple in Jerusalem were adding the name of Jesus to their blacklist. They could not close their eyes to the restlessness apparent on the shores of the Lake of Galilee. They had emerged as winners in the turn of events which brought about the imprisonment near the Dead Sea of that dangerous prophet John the Baptist, and now they turned their attention to still another dangerous character, whom the yokels of Galilee were beginning to acclaim as John's successor. Didn't this same fellow in fact carry on during the festival of Booths openly in disregard for the sabbath day of rest?

Every move of Jesus, his popularity in the towns around the lake, the hopes and dreams which the inhabitants had fixed on him—one thing after another—all was reported to Jerusalem. This intelligence came from their own agents whom they had established in Tiberias, the biggest city on the lake. The agents' overlord in Jerusalem was the high priest Caiaphas, a son-in-law to the former high priest Annas (in Hebrew, *Hananiah*), whose influence had prevailed with the Roman governor of Judea to ratify the son-in-law's appointment to his eminent position.

The office of high priest, equivalent to being primate over all the clergy, had formerly been the hereditary privilege of the Hasmonean dynasty, but following the abolition of the dynasty the spiritual primacy was determined by election from the powerful priestly nobility. The specific function of the high priest was to preside over the sacrifices and other religious services provided in the temple, but the high priest was also responsible to Rome for other matters beyond the religious ceremonies. The office therefore included the high priest's duty as presiding officer in the Sanhedrin, the supreme administrative council in matters religious and secular.

The Sanhedrin, including its presiding officer, consisted of seventy-one members, who fell into three distinct groups. The first group drew its membership from all the former high priests and from those noble families eligible for election to high priest. The second group was a mixture of elders drawn from the lay aristocracy (all of whom, like the first group, adhered to the sect of the Sadducees) and from scions of other affluent families. The last group were the doctors of the Law (the scribes), and these came mostly from the more plebeian strata of society.

All questions, religious or civil, were decided on the basis of Jewish Law (Torah), and even Pilate the governor respected the council's autonomy. What Rome did not allow to the Sanhedrin was the right to inflict capital punishment.

To speak more precisely, on this last point there are two theories. I intend to consider the matter in more detail later on, although nobody knows today whether the Sanhedrin lacked all power of life and death or whether the council was merely prohibited by Rome from carrying out the execution of political criminals. Some scholars hold that the Sanhedrin at the time had no life-and-death power whatsoever, while others say (based on a passage in the Acts of the Apostles, beginning from Chapter 6 verse 8, where the Sanhedrin sentences a culprit charged with blasphemy to be stoned to death) that the Sanhedrin actually had authority to administer capital punishment, but that the authority did not extend to crimes in the political order. This question of whether or not the Sanhedrin had authority over the death penalty is important background material to the legal proceedings at the trial of Jesus, which we must consider later on.

In either event, back in Jerusalem the Sanhedrin, in control of Caiaphas and his father-in-law Annas, was keeping a watchful eye on Jesus up in Galilee.

Wherever Jesus went, the numbers who gathered to hear him speak increased amazingly. His fame spread from town to town. People waited enthusiastically to welcome him with the disciples as they traveled about on foot or by boat. His close disciples also rapidly increased. Their number is not to be restricted to the select group referred to as the twelve apostles. The numeral twelve had its own symbolic meaning in the Jewish way of thought. Nevertheless the Twelve, those whose names appear on lists supplied in the Gospels, did constitute a nucleus for the fast-growing corps of disciples. (There is however some slight discrepancy concerning the names of the disciples as they are listed in the several Gospels.)

Jesus by this time was free of the religious community of John the Baptist and was working independently. He no longer carried out in Galilee the rite of baptism which John had performed at the River Jordan. Jesus always maintained his deep respect and affection for the precursor, saying of him: "He is far more than a prophet. . . . Among those born of women there has risen no one greater than John the Baptist" (Matthew 11:7,11), but immediately, in speaking to his own disciples, he added clearly: "Yet he who is least in the kingdom of heaven is greater than John." What Jesus rejected was the forbidding ascetical image which characterized the community of John the Baptist, because in the heart of Jesus already lived the God of love and the love of God instead of the God of judgment and the God of wrath, the God of retribution as John's community conceived of him.

Yet how was Jesus to bear witness to this God of love for all the people? Obviously the existential condition of mankind favored a God of vengeance rather than a God of love. It is understandable how in the long Old Testament tradition people spoke continually of their feeling of awe toward God, and of the silence of God, far more than about their love of God. How was Jesus to affirm his positive attitude toward the paradox between the obvious facts of life and the God of love? People in suffering, people in sickness, people in tears could not consider themselves except as being estranged from God, while the other people beholding them could sense nothing underlying their sad plight except the wrath and punishment of God.

> Blessed are the poor in spirit,
>   for theirs is the kingdom of heaven.
> Blessed are those who mourn,
>   for they shall be comforted.

Jesus realized that his own life-work lay in solving this problem. How were men and women to discover within the harsh reality of human life the genuine love of God? The task which he took upon himself in the wilderness of Judea now occupied his heart completely. Jesus felt that God had sent him into the world to answer this question, and he realized that many painful obstacles must be overcome to carry out his mission. By reading between the lines in the Bible we can see the figure of Jesus standing near the shore of the Lake of Galilee, completely alone, even when surrounded by his disciples and by the crowds.

The scribes and the Pharisees, arriving from Jerusalem, began their investigation of the words and deeds of Jesus by mixing with the crowds. The overwhelming popularity of Jesus prevented their seizing him directly, but these agents were under pressure to discover any scrap of warrantable evidence against him (Mark 12:12). They had been dispatched by the Sanhedrin precisely to uncover definite grounds on which to base an indictment.

The wranglings between Jesus and the Pharisees, of frequent occurrence in the Bible, seem at a glance to be no more than casual quarrels, yet behind these altercations lay the unseen antagonism between Jesus and the Sanhedrin in Jerusalem. The debates must be read against the background of the questioning of the Pharisees and scribes who were, in fact, investigators dispatched for a purpose— they were spies.

These men were adroit in the art of debate, since through a long period of history they had engaged unceasingly in discussing the various interpretations of articles in the Law. They knew precisely how to lay a booby trap and where to set a snare. They infiltrated the crowds, from where they heckled Jesus into disputing them, in order to educe convincing evidence that Jesus was a heretic or a dangerous enemy of Rome.

More than any other book in the Bible, the Gospel of Mark presents the liveliest account of the altercations between Jesus and the inquisitors. The questions of the inquisitors tend to concentrate on trying to show that Jesus was possibly a heretic who defied the Law binding upon all Jews. Although the Sadducees and the Pharisees between themselves were occasionally at loggerheads, they were always in agreement about the central importance of the temple, and they were of one mind about strictly preserving the Law as bequeathed to them by the forefathers.

In their minds, Jesus was nothing but a blasphemer of the Law, as shown during the festival of Booths when he disregarded the inviolable sabbath rest by tending the sick and the lame at the Pool of Bethesda.

A group of Pharisees, with some doctors of the Law who had come from Jerusalem, met him and noticed that some of his disciples were eating their food with "defiled" hands—in other words, without washing them. (For . . . Jews in general never eat without washing their hands, in obedience to an old-established tradition. . . . And there are other points on which they have a traditional rule to maintain, for example, washing of cups and jugs and copper bowls.) Accordingly, these Pharisees and the lawyers asked him, "Why do your disciples not conform to the ancient tradition, but eat their food with defiled hands?" (Mark 7:1).

On a sabbath, while he was going through the grain fields, his disciples plucked and ate some ears of grain, rubbing them in their hands. But some of the Pharisees said, "Why are you doing what is not lawful to do on the sabbath?" (Luke 6:1).

These spontaneous arguments seem to be recorded rather casually, yet they do illustrate the sort of grilling directed at Jesus by the inquisitors from Jerusalem. If we are inclined to interpret the passages as merely casual squabbles, that is because we fail to appreciate the profound reverence of the Jews of that time for the sabbath and for the Law. Even in our own day and age, foreign tourists in Israel are prohibited on the sabbath from drinking alcoholic beverages in their hotels, and there are even times in Jerusalem when foreigners have been pelted with stones for driving a car on the sabbath. This can help us better to imagine the angry amazement of the Pharisees and the scribes when, after they vehemently criticized the acts of Jesus in violation of the sabbath, they heard him answer: "The sabbath was made for the sake of man and not man for the sabbath." We have no longer any reason to wonder just why "they discussed among themselves what they might do to Jesus" (Luke 6:11).

Having detected the odor of blasphemy by their assessing the opinions of Jesus against the measure of their own values, the inquisitors then began to move around and pass the word that Jesus was a "bastard" [Hebrew: *mamzer*] and a "wine-bibber and a glutton" —anything to tear down the public opinion which favored him. After all, the Law concerning unbelievers decreed that if a suspicion of apostasy attached itself to anyone, the culprit's origin was to be investigated, because bastards (the offspring of an invalid marriage or of illicit sex) were thought to have a proclivity for treason and a tendency to blaspheme God. So long as a base-born person lived in accord with the divine will, he was not to be affronted, but should he turn apostate, his illegitimate origin was to be mercilessly exposed (Leviticus 21:10ff.). Furthermore, contemptuous epithets like "glutton" and "drunkard" also carried the innuendo of illegitimate birth (Deuteronomy 22:21).

Yet the common people paid no attention to the mudslinging, not as yet. In the towns everywhere they flocked around Jesus with great enthusiasm, and the inquisitors were helpless (Mark 12:22).

Then there was a switch in strategy. Since the populace could not recognize in Jesus a blasphemer against the Law, the inquisitors then took up the task of trying to prove that Jesus was a dangerous character who stirred up anti-Roman feelings in the population around the Lake of Galilee, on which ground they could proceed to lodge a complaint against him before Pilate the governor or before King Herod Antipas. John the Baptist, entangled by a similar strategem, had been arrested and already had been punished. The inquisitors tried laying a similar trap for Jesus. Taking pains to assume an air of modesty in order to impress the crowd, they posed another question to him: "Master, you are an honest man, we know; you teach in all honesty the way of life that God requires, truckling to no man whoever he may be."

A moment of quiet swept the crowd, and when all had perked their ears, they could hear the snappish question: "Are we or are we not permitted to pay taxes to the Roman emperor?"

If Jesus said that taxes ought to be paid to the Roman emperor, the nationalists in the crowd would be disappointed. If he said that taxes ought not to be paid, his enemies could interpret his statement as demagogic agitation. Caught in this ingenious trap, how was Jesus to answer?

The crowd waited, holding their breath. Jesus asked to be shown a single silver coin, and then he inquired whose head was engraved on the coin. Being told that it was the head of the Roman emperor, Jesus went on to say: "Then pay Caesar what is due to Caesar, and pay God what is due to God." The inquisitors were at a loss for words to rebut him. They could find no solid evidence to prove him an anti-Roman agitator, and they were also failing still to create in the minds of the people an image of Jesus as a religious heretic. Thus they were forced to slink away.

Jesus was on his own. What caused him anguish was not the tenacious hounding by inquisitors. Trivialities did not upset him. The cause of his sadness lay in all the towns around the lake—the only world which he knew at the time—and there were too many tears in that world. From the biblical accounts of his Galilean ministry we get acquainted with the sick and crippled people who appear. We know about a mother who lost her son, a father who lost his little girl. We get to know the hated tax collectors and the prostitutes when they enter the scene. But the sad situation was not confined to these individuals who are specifically mentioned, for we also feel squirming around in the background the presence of those vast numbers of unhappy people whom the biblical authors do not describe individually.

Jesus went on foot from town to town. He moved by boat from one shore of the lake to another. The winter passed and spring came visiting again. The lake was at peace, basking in sunshine, and along the shores the red anemone bloomed everywhere. On the far-off horizon towered the snow-capped peak of Mount Hermon.

Springtime in Galilee! Was nature anywhere more benign! Nature was nought but the flaming forth of the love of God and the God of love, as Jesus in his own mind had come to image God. Yet it was heartbreaking in the extreme, this being forced to witness the harsh realities of human life within the towns and hamlets. What could he do to reconcile the suffering of human existence with the existence of the God of love?

A glance at the "miracle narratives" helps us understand how greatly Jesus, in the circle of his disciples, exerted himself in trying to help these wretched people. He went even to places where the outcast lepers huddled together in their own groups. People sick with malaria struck terror in the hearts of others who supposed them to be "possessed by the devils," but there is no doubt that the footsteps of Jesus moved out to the hovels in which the sick were forced to stay at a distance from the towns. Jesus could not agree that the God of love had forsaken these otherwise forsaken ones. Certain places where the sick lived in their isolation were within seeing distance of the sanitized city of Tiberias downshore. But Jesus never entertained a thought to entering Tiberias. He had no interest in the self-complacent people there, the self-righteous and the affluent. The interest of Jesus extended to the ones who wept for the harsh realities of life: the sick and the lame crawling out of the huts which lay squeezed together beyond the poverty-stricken towns and hamlets.

His heart ached at the sight. Love and sympathy flowed from him like blood from a deep wound. We in our own hearts know how we are attracted to glamorous and beautiful people and how we easily close our eyes to those who are filthy and ugly. It was different with Jesus, whose predilection was for the lepers and the harlots whom others despised. Consider the unfortunate characters appearing in the miracle stories. The burden of pain from all of them falls on the narrow shoulders of Jesus. At such a time he must have groaned within himself: "My God, my God, why have you abandoned me?"

He had frequent occasion to voice on behalf of these unhappy souls in Galilee the words of this prayer from the Book of Psalms, which later he pronounced from the gibbet of his own cross.

The Jerusalem spies were by no means about to surrender their cause. They understood well how fickle the nature of public opinion was. By and by would come a time for the crowds to sober up from their madness. The hour would come for illusion to fade, for passion to cool. It was simply that the common people of Galilee were attaching their own dreams on the person of Jesus. But the disparity between the real Jesus and the Jesus of their dreams would not take long to emerge. Time was on the side of the spies, who could afford to be patient.

At first the people near the lake had looked upon Jesus as a successor to John the Baptist. They had fixed on Jesus, the favorite disciple of John, the respect and the support which they bore for the prophet who had met his tragic death in the citadel of Machaerus. But when they observed that Jesus did not continue the practice of baptizing in the manner of John, their expectations for Jesus shifted direction. A few voices were heard to speculate that Jesus with the right kind of popular support might be just the man to try for something big. Indelible in their memories was the revolt which had broken out in the Galilean town of Gamala thirty years before. A man of Gamala named Judas had recruited a band of supporters with whom he seized Sepphoris, a Roman arsenal two miles north of Nazareth, as the first move in restoring its glory to the conquered land of the Jews. Thanks to the Roman general Varus, however, it wasn't long before the insurgents were given an opportunity to choose the death of heroes in preference to base surrender. Their heroic spirit then became the heritage of a secret fraternity called the Zealots. It was the province of Galilee that was mother's womb to the Zealot party. There is no mistake in what Fosdick wrote in his book *The Man from Nazareth*: "That some of them [the Zealots] thought he might become their leader in armed resistance against Rome seems evident. This was their main need—a rousing personality who would precipitate the general unrest into definite insurrection."

People like the Zealots, and others in favor of a Galilean revolt, at least had reason to imagine how the tremendous popularity of Jesus might be used to advantage in their cause.

Jesus knew well that eyes like these were looking at him from the crowds all around him—and not only from the crowds, for even in the tight circle of his own disciples Jesus had Simon, who was formerly linked with the Zealots. He had Peter too. He also had Judas. He knew how the minds of these men were operating as they listened to their master speaking.

Jesus determined the attitude for himself to adopt vis-à-vis these disciples of his. Being their fellow Galilean he was sensitive to the patriots' singleness of purpose. He was fully aware of the yearnings and the anguish of the Jews who had been oppressed so long by the tyranny of foreign conquerors. He was at odds with them only on the question of how to satisfy their anguished yearnings. He said to them at a later time, "All those who take the sword will perish by the sword" (Matthew 26:52). And on another occasion he quietly laid it down: "My kingdom is not of this world." But that all came later, and during the springtime in Galilee he contented himself with moderate words of caution.

> God makes his sun to rise on the good and bad alike, and sends the rain on the honest and the dishonest.

> Love your enemies, do good to those who hate you, and pray for your persecutors.

> Beware of false prophets, who come to you in sheep's clothing but inwardly are ravenous wolves.

We don't know how these sayings of Jesus were received by the crowds that pressed about him. Most likely the crowds were unable to penetrate the meaning of what he was saying to them. Not even his close disciples could fathom his true intent.

The feast of Passover for the year 31 was not far away. It was traditional to believe that when the messianic Savior of the Jews appeared, it would be at Passover time. The Roman chains which bound the Jews had been pulled even tighter since the Passover of the previous year, producing the backlash effect of inciting more and more Jewish patriotism with the steady approach of another Passover. Just at this juncture occurred in Jerusalem the incident of Pilate the governor's carrying out the death penalty on a number of Galileans (Luke 13:1), on top of which came the accidental collapse of the tower of Siloam, resulting in eighteen fatalities. In the disturbing atmosphere of these disasters people were ready for something still more startling. Little by little up near the Lake of Galilee they began to see in Jesus the one who could make something really big happen. Certain ones were emerging in the crowd to suggest that the nation's long-waited Messiah was Jesus himself.

The climactic moment of the Galilean ministry turned out to be the event on a day when "the Passover, the feast of the Jews, was near at hand" (John 6:4), when the people, seeing Jesus head toward the mountains, gathered around him there in tremendous numbers (John 6:4). During the afternoon Jesus spoke of many things, and when the sun was already near the horizon, the crowd still gave no sign of breaking up. When Jesus heard the disciples say that they had prepared no more than two fish and five loaves of bread for their own use, he organized the crowd into a number of smaller groups, directing them all to sit comfortably on the fresh grass, and it is reported next that he accomplished the marvelous act of feeding everybody by multiplying the few loaves of bread and the two fish into more than 5,000 servings.

The Gospels recount great numbers of miracles performed by Jesus, but the only one recorded in all four of the Gospels is the miracle of serving this meal. Many Bible scholars relate this miracle story to the Old Testament's Second Book of Kings (4:42-44), where the prophet Elisha is said to have multiplied twenty loaves of bread to feed one hundred men—the scholars then going on to indicate that the Old Testament story is prototype to the story in the four Gospels.

My own interest centers on a point brought up in John's Gospel: that the events portrayed in this particular miracle story occurred on a day near the feast of Passover. Passover was preeminently the festival that nurtured the emotional ethnocentrism of the Jews, and the event in the story came on a day near Passover. The event came at the moment when the popularity of Jesus happened to coincide with the heightened intensity in the people's dream of the Messiah's coming, the advent of their Savior who would expel the conqueror and restore to them the Kingdom of Judah. The figure cited of five thousand men is perhaps the evangelist's hyperbole, but there is no doubt that the people surrounding Jesus on the mountain made up a vast multitude. At the end of John's account of the day's proceedings the author flatly observes an amazing fact which the other evangelists fail to note, namely that "the people were about to come and take him by force to make him king, but Jesus withdrew again to the hills by himself."

The famished crowd of five thousand men lacking provisions represent the whole Jewish nation, while the act of Jesus in sharing with each of them his sustenance in the nature of love is the essential point in this miracle story, paralleling as it does the action of Jesus during the famous Last Supper—except that behind the miracle story is contained the historical fact of how Jesus flatly refused to become the "earthly Messiah" desired by the crowd.

If we keep this point clearly in mind as we thoughtfully read of still another event near the Lake of Galilee, namely the well-known Sermon on the Mount, we cannot miss a remarkable connection between the two. A similar introductory formula is used in all of the Gospels to set the scene for both the miracle story of the loaves and fishes and for the Sermon on the Mount. Although Matthew says that the Sermon on the Mount took place literally "on a mountain," and that the distribution of food was at "a lonely place," yet, taken together, both expressions can be interpreted as a place away from any town. Also, the two events equally take place in the presence of the disciples together with a vast crowd. We can hardly miss concluding that the two stories speak of events which occurred on one and the same day. We can't escape thinking how the stories are related to each other.

When the two narratives are laid side by side, we see the total situation emerge. On the afternoon of a day near the feast of Passover the enormous crowd assembling on the mountain was all at one in yelling for Jesus to stand up then and there for the kingdom of Judah. They shouted out how they would follow him, if only he agreed to be their leader. At the approach of Passover the crowd was already keyed up to the nationalistic spirit celebrated in the festival. The Gospels do not explicitly record any particulars about the avid passion of the crowd, but the words of Jesus in John 18:36 strongly imply that it was available.

The crowd waited for their answer from Jesus. The band of his disciples were seated close to him, and no doubt the spies of the inquisition were unobtrusively infiltrated among the people. The disciples and the spies both waited breathlessly to see how Jesus would respond.

He did not respond. Conceivably he took occasion to cite some words from the sixty-first chapter of the Book of Isaiah: "The Lord has anointed me to bring good tidings to the poor; he has sent me to bind up the broken-hearted" (Isaiah 61:1-3).

Then people heard the voice of Jesus coming to them in a steady stream on the wings of the wind:

> Blessed are the poor in spirit,
>   for theirs is the kingdom of heaven.
> Blessed are the meek,
>   for they shall inherit the earth.
> Blessed are they that mourn,
>   for they shall be comforted.
> Blessed are the pure in heart,
>   for they shall see God.

His voice moved across the flocks of sheep grazing on the gentle slopes, through the patches of trees casting their reflection in the lake, through the groves and across the scarlet anemones in bloom along the shore. The lake itself lay calm under sunny skies, and tiny boats were floating in the distance.

A commotion stirred through the crowd. They never dreamed that Jesus would react to their shouted expectations with an amazing answer like this. The rabbinical Judaism on which they had been raised was by no means in total disregard of the notion of love, but the rabbis had not inculcated this ideal of love as the value par excellence to ignite their religious fervor. There had been no thought of exalting to such an extreme the value of those who are poor in spirit, and meek, or who mourn and are pure in heart. What on earth was Jesus attempting to imply in words like these?

> But I say to you—Jesus poured it on—love your enemies, do good to those who hate you. Bless those who curse you. Pray for those who abuse you. To him who strikes you on the cheek, offer the other also. From him who takes away your coat do not withhold your cloak as well.

They had never received any instruction that touched on this sort of love from either the doctors of the Law or the priests. None of the prophets, including John the Baptist, had ever delivered a discourse on love to match this one by Jesus. His principle of love was directly opposed to all casuist commentaries regarding the letter of the Law. The teaching of Jesus demanded of men and women an impossible standard of sincerity in heart and soul, of purity, honesty, and self-denial:

> Give to every one who begs from you, and of him who takes away your goods do not ask them again. And as you wish that men would do to you, do so to them. If you love those who love you, what credit is that to you? . . . Is that the way to act for sons of the Most High?

The spirit of forgiveness . . . the spirit of sacrifice . . . this teaching was altogether in contrast to the prudential maxims concerning success in life which they had always heard read to them from the sapiential books, or had heard from the injunctions of the Pharisees. It was a summons to love which lies perhaps beyond the power of mere human earthlings to attempt.

It shook the crowd. Now they had their unequivocal answer from Jesus—flat refusal. The crowd had expected no such response to their nationalistic clamor. They sat there disillusioned. There was simply no reconciling the image of Jesus, on which they had centered their dreams, and the reality of Jesus when he delivered to them his own call for action. Jesus turned down the popular demand in words which have since become famous. People got to their feet and began to move down the hill. Embittered by their disappointment, some of them moved away spewing obscenities. Others were shouting in anger. The only ones to show any sign of being satisfied were the spies from Jerusalem. The wheel had come full turn, as they expected that eventually it would, and this was the day to mark the beginning of the end—the people's disillusionment with Jesus and their subsequent disaffection.

6 "THE SON OF MAN HAS NOWHERE TO LAY HIS HEAD"

BEING disillusioned by Jesus was not limited to the common people from the lake country who happened that day to be part of the crowd around Jesus on the mountain. We can readily imagine how there was more than a little wavering even within the circle of his own disciples.

The number of these close disciples had grown appreciably in the six months Jesus had been preaching. They were more numerous than the tightly knit band of men known to the world as the twelve apostles. The number twelve was a sacrosanct and symbolic numeral in Jewish life. In fact, however, those who had joined the company of his disciples exceed that number by far. They did not derive from the affluent class of society, but were apt to be more like fishermen or tax collectors. In the beginning they did not give up their daily employment on becoming disciples, and only later did some of them leave Galilee and stay in the company of the master on his journeys.

Among these Galileans, faithful religious Jews, were some who belonged to the party of the Zealots, but even those who had never joined the Zealots were strong in their patriotism and ethnic awareness. No doubt each one had his or her own personal reasons for remaining close to Jesus, but deep in their hearts they all held to a sentiment little different from the sentiment of the crowd—the urge to make Jesus a nationalistic leader—all of which is made clear from the frank confession of one of them: "But for our part we had been hoping that he might be the man destined to liberate Israel" (Luke 24:21). Their hopes took a practical turn with the gradually rising tide of the master's popularity around the Lake of Galilee, but when their master squelched these earthbound hopes with his Sermon on the Mount, there was considerable wavering even among the inner circle.

The disillusionment of the crowd, the wavering of the disciples—the inquisitors could hardly fail to perceive what had happened. If Jesus had played along with the fervent demand of the crowd assembled on the mountain, the spies were prepared to finger him, and to hasten his arrest as a demagogic agitator by reporting the facts immediately to Herod Antipas and also to Pilate, the governor of Judea, but the declaration which actually came from Jesus was directly contrary to what the crowd had expected. The Gospels show that not only not on this occasion but never once during his Galilean ministry did Jesus utter a single word to suggest that he was the Messiah, that is, the one who would liberate Israel. Stauffer says: "The fundamental and incontestable fact is that the idea of being the 'Messiah' can be found nowhere in the collection of the sayings of Jesus [i.e., nowhere in the historical materials assembled before the New Testament was written, and consisting of a collection of the words spoken by Jesus]. The same applies to any similar messianic titles like son of David, or king of Israel, or king of the Jews. In other words the historical materials called the sayings of Jesus contain not a single word of any messianic self-description." Stauffer says in another place that "the historical contents of the sayings of Jesus lead us to conclude that Jesus never chose to refer to himself as the Messiah. '

The surveillance team had failed to expose any evidence that

Jesus was a popular agitator, but they were in position that day to observe the disillusionment in the faces of the crowd and the first signs of wavering among the disciples. The spies were eager to report the events of the day back to the Jerusalem Sanhedrin, and they got together immediately to discuss among themselves all possible alternatives. The Sermon on the Mount was a happy event to these men of long experience in crowd psychology. For when a fanatic crowd feels that its own high hopes are betrayed, it has a way of swinging around to hating its former idol with a vehemence equal to the measure of its disillusionment. The spies were well acquainted with the ficklemindedness of the rabble.

But Jesus, too, was astutely aware of this psychology of the common man. Throughout his half a year of ministry, from the moment people began to press about him, when he was received with shouts of joy in one town after another, he sensed a premonition of the day to come when these men and women would reject him.

The God of love, the love of God—the words come easy. The most difficult thing is to bear witness in some tangible way to the truth of the words. In many cases love is actually powerless. Love has in itself no immediate tangible benefits. We are therefore hard put to find where the love of God can be, hidden behind tangible realities which rather suggest that God does not exist, or that he never speaks, or that he is angry.

During these six months Jesus could not escape his poignant impression that the people after all sought nothing but utilitarian benefits. He preached purely the love of God and the God of love, but those inclined to hear his actual message were very few indeed. Even his disciples failed to catch the meaning of what he said. The disciples, like the common people, had come to him seeking nothing more than worldly profit, not love. The blind asked for nothing but to regain their sight, the lame to restore the use of their legs, the lepers to dry their purulent sores.

The copious miracle stories in the Synoptic Gospels as well as in John bring home to us the sad fact that the crowd sought nothing but prodigies from Jesus—a consideration far more significant than the threadbare question of whether Jesus did or did not perform the miracles. Behind these miracle stories we sense the lonely figure of Jesus himself, standing quietly in the crowd of people demanding nothing but corporeal wonders.

Jesus did not reject these kinds of sick and crippled people. On the contrary, the Gospels clearly relate how with his disciples he went to the valley of the lepers, whom other people detested, and how he visited the hovel of a man who suffered the agonies of malaria. The lepers in those days used to shave their heads, they wore distinctive dress, and they were put away at a distance from any towns or villages. They called out a warning when anybody approached. Jesus walked through the mountain coves and the gullies where these forsaken lepers were forced to live. He wanted to restore their healthy bodies. He wanted to restore to the blind the use of their eyes. He wanted to make the lame walk. He wanted to bring back a lost child to a bereaved mother.

But a look of sadness came to his eyes when he could not do it. He held the hand of a leper, or a lame man, and he pleaded earnestly his desire to take upon himself their misery and pain. He asked for a share in their suffering, a chance to be partners with them. But the lepers and the cripples were hoping only to be healed. They came pleading to Jesus: "Cure us! Cure us!"

What are we to make of these exclamations of Jesus, which the Gospels have left us along with the miracle narratives? "You seek for a sign, but no sign shall be given except the sign of the prophet Jonah" (Matthew 12:39). "Why does this generation ask for a sign?" (Mark 8:12). "Unless you see signs and wonders you will not believe" (John 4:48). "Blessed are those who have not seen me and yet believe" (John 20:29).

The realistic pathos in these words of Jesus, preserved for us in the Gospels, comes from the fact that the people appearing before him were looking not for "love" but for signs and wonders. They wanted only quick and tangible benefits.

The backstage maneuvering of the spies began to have its effect, little by little. Disquiet and wavering were taking root in the minds of the disciples, even though they were not as yet prepared to abandon their master. The crowds in Galilee who had flocked about him suddenly found themselves sobering up from their binge of fanatic enthusiasm. In their eyes Jesus began to look like "a prophet of forlorn hope." The operations of the spies had gradually engendered in people's minds a new image of Jesus as a "weakling" and a "washout." Then at last the summer changed to fall and the time arrived for the fields of wheat around the lake to mature into sallow straw.

From this season forward his opportunities for private prayer became more frequent for Jesus. Although as yet he confided nothing about it to his disciples, the heart of Jesus was preoccupied by an interior struggle, to match in its intensity the lonely struggle which he had experienced in the wilderness of Judea. He had faith in the love of God. He was so moved by this love that wherever he saw the pitiable men and women of Galilee, he wanted to share their suffering. He could not think, since God was Love itself, that God would forsake these people. Yet no one could appreciate the mystery of God's love. The people by the Lake of Galilee eventually fell away from Jesus because they demanded material benefits rather than love, and therefore Jesus prayed earnestly to God for guidance to discern what best to do in this situation.

"My God, my God, why have you abandoned me?" How many times this anguished verse from the Psalms must have come to his lips. Heartbreaking loneliness carved his face in lines that made him look older than his years, and still the disciples failed to understand. Just as on a later occasion in the Garden of Gethsemane they were impervious to their master's bloodlike sweat, so at this time too they were blind to his interior suffering.

The chilly atmosphere with regard to Jesus began to pervade even towns like Capernaum and Chorazin and Bethsaida, the very places where he had been so warmly received in the spring and during the summer. The "weakling," the "washout"—the jibes began coming with sardonic smiles from the mouths of people in those places too. The disaffection in the towns deeply saddened him (Matthew 11:21).

We can suppose that it was precisely this coolness in the atmosphere which moved Jesus to leave the area around the lake and go back to Nazareth. It was not a full year since he had departed from

Nazareth and settled by the lake with his mother and her few intimates, but the unfavorable change in conditions prompted him to return.

The inquisitors had apparently acted beforehand in getting the news to Nazareth. The people living there greeted Jesus and his company with eyes of suspicion. Now that he was back, not even his kinsmen made any effort to offer him the hospitality of their homes. Quite the opposite—now that he had returned to them only after being hounded out of the towns and villages by the lake, they were all for taking him to task for his lack of responsibility in having deserted them in the first place by running off to the wilderness of Judea (Mark 3:21).

In Nazareth the inquisitors again challenged him to debate. They went so far as to charge that his preaching was not by the inspiration of God, but the work of the evil spirit. Some of the inhabitants did come asking him for a miracle, like the people of the towns near the lake, except that their eyes had a look of contemptuous curiosity rather than real expectation. Seeing Jesus perform no wonders, they were carried away in anger, going so far as to take him up the rocky elevation south of the town, from where they tried to throw him over the cliff (Luke 4:29).

When we patch together all the scattered references in the Gospels to unpleasantries in Nazareth, we grasp the extent of the hard feelings which greeted Jesus after returning there from the Lake of Galilee. Incurring such animosity and opposition even from his kinsmen and former acquaintances, Jesus observed that the "foxes have their holes, the birds of the air have their nests, but the Son of Man has nowhere to lay his head" (Luke 9:58). We hear these sad words coming from Jesus, and our own heartstrings quiver in poignant sympathy. Saying with regret that "no prophet is acceptable in his own country," Jesus went away again from his own home town.

"After this many of his disciples withdrew and no longer went about with him."

This breaking up of his disciples, mentioned only in John 6:66 occurred most likely at about this time. The disciples who remained with him were reduced, it seems, to only a few. It is also written in

John's Gospel that Jesus turned to them and sadly asked: "Do you also want to leave me?"

Those who had chosen to depart were doubtless persuaded that they could no longer afford to entrust their dreams to Jesus. Most of them still considered him a teacher fully capable of hypnotizing the mass of people, and they still had cause to regard him as a leader worthy to replace John the Baptist; but when they saw in one place after another, both on the shore by the lake and again at Nazareth, that the people were turning away, these disciples lost the heart to follow him. In their estimation also, Jesus had become forever a "do-nothing" and a "weakling."

For those disciples who chose to remain with Jesus, we find it hard to imagine what could be brewing in their minds and hearts. When he asked them sadly "Do you also want to leave me?" Peter's response is on record: "Lord, to whom shall we go? You have the words of eternal life"; but this response may not have been delivered actually at that time, and the choice of words may be no more than a reflection of the kerygma (the confession of faith) emanating from the primitive Christian Church, all of which is later development. Yet the fact remains that those disciples who stayed on in spite of their misgivings, in spite of the wavering in their own minds, had found it impossible to imitate the break that was made by those who had departed. Certainly, even the ones who remained with Jesus had lost much of their hope in him. But whatever the explanation, they could not bring themselves to desert their powerless master. Had they had it within themselves to defect, they would have chosen to do so. And yet for nothing in the world could they bring themselves to break away from Jesus, who was now an outcast, who now stood isolated.

Very likely, the weaker Jesus appeared to be, the more they unconsciously felt what unspeakable regret and loneliness might afterward be theirs, if they too were to forsake him.

After leaving Nazareth, Jesus and the few disciples still with him moved through the dreary hill country, always on foot, from one town to some other neighboring town. The disciples were exhausted, near the point of losing hope entirely. Jesus continued his prayers to God. Often he spoke the sad lament: "My God, my

God, why have you abandoned me?" And while he did so, he began to detect in his inner ear the voice of God calling him, and he became aware of how hard it was going to be for him to obey that voice. The disciples still were totally unaware of the master's intense inner struggle.

We don't really know just how many souls made up the paltry handful remaining with him. We surmise that the number was somewhat larger than the twelve whom the Gospels mention by name. We have, for example, the well-known case of Judas Iscariot, who arrived at open defection but only later and in Jerusalem, and it is safe to suppose that in the meantime he was not the only new defector. We don't know the names of all the disciples, but the ones we do know are Peter and Andrew, James and John, Matthew (Levi) and Thomas, Philip and Bartholomew, James (the son of Alpheus) and Thaddeus, Simon and Judas Iscariot. These names are listed in the Gospels of Matthew and Mark, but Luke mentions a Jude, the son of James, in place of Thaddeus. This Jude is not to be confused with the Judas who later betrayed Jesus, and Jude and Thaddeus are names referring most likely to one and the same man.

There is something baffling in the picture of these dozen men or so, silently walking behind Jesus of Nazareth, their bone-tired feet carrying them into the lonely hill country stretching before them toward the north. I said earlier that the disciples did not belong to the priestly caste of Jewry, nor were they men of formal education like the doctors of the Law. Neither did they come from the moneyed upper class of people living in Tiberias. They were in fact a group of men, fishers or tax collectors and the like, from the lower middle class, all of whom (except Judas) had been living in the towns and villages near the Lake of Galilee until they came to know Jesus. The words written by Paul more than twenty years later to describe the early Christian church at Corinth can well be applied to these disciples too: "Not many of you were wise according to worldly standards, not many were powerful, not many were of noble birth."

It would be a mistake to suppose that these men became disciples of Jesus only after coming to appreciate his ideal of love. As I have said time and again, most of them simply joined the inner circle of disciples for the same reasons that drew the big crowds he encountered at the Lake of Galilee. No one can claim that the disciples, being men of simple heart, did not possess that sense of right and wrong which is part of being a devout Jewish believer, nor that as individuals they were totally free of vainglory and personal ambition. The authors of the New Testament were unable to hide the fact that the disciples in the end were also wanting in courage and will-power. When Jesus finally was arrested, they not only disowned him, but it seems clear that his disciples gave first thought to their own safety, then begged for clemency from the Sanhedrin. In that sense they were ordinary folk, and weaklings at that, like most of us.

They positively misunderstood Jesus. Not only did they mistake him, but also they never considered him as being the "Son of God." Yet they persevered in dragging their feet along the road on the heels of their woebegone master, even after so many others had deserted. Was it some kind of inexpressible purity and melancholy in the eyes of Jesus? In our own lives there can be an occasion where we cross paths with another person, when the very thought of the other's purity of heart can make us painfully conscious of our own meanness. Maybe with these disciples, at the time in question, Jesus still was that kind of master, and the only thing which held their little band together was a feeling that they would be haunted by lonely regret for the rest of their lives if they were to desert him now.

In spite of any such feeling, however, they, too, turned traitor at the end. (Treachery was not confined to Judas Iscariot, for all the disciples still remaining had a hand in it—a matter I intend to enlarge upon in a later chapter.) The disciples were, so to speak, pretty much like the rest of us after all—a collection of no-good cowards and weaklings.

Nevertheless, all of a sudden, following on the death of Jesus, their eyes were opened. Weaklings and cowards they had been, but nothing could intimidate them after that, not even death. They never flinched at any physical terror. For Jesus' sake they stoutly bore the rigors of distant journeys, and stoutly they held out under persecution. Peter underwent martyrdom in Rome about the year A.D. 61. Andrew was put to death by starvation in the Greek city of

Patras. Simon, who had belonged to the Zealots, is said to have been killed for preaching Jesus in the city of Suanis, and Bartholomew was flayed alive and then hung on a cross at Albanopolis.

What in the world effected so marvelous a turnaround in them, so amazing a change? Was it no more than some trace of influence picked up from Jesus, who himself had accomplished nothing, that made his disciples act as they did? The usual way in reading the New Testament is to keep the spotlight on Jesus, but if we go back and read again in a way to see the disciples play leading roles, then a singular theme emerges—how weaklings, cowards, and no-goods metamorphose into characters of unshakable faith. But the real cause behind the disciples' marvelous change, this theme set out for us in the New Testament, can even be termed an enigma.

Be that as it may, by autumn of that same year it appears that Jesus and his disciples had executed a wandering journey which carried them, literally with "no place whereon to lay their heads," from the southern part of Galilee (Luke 7:11) as far as the land of Tyre and Sidon (Mark 7:24, 31). Our uncertainty about place names in their itinerary is in itself a kind of evidence of how painful was the memory of those days for the few disciples who survived and who later provided the material which found its way into the Bible. The interior struggle of Jesus was beyond the disciples' ability to comprehend, and Jesus himself was avoiding public attention. We can easily infer that the reduced number of the disciples continued growing smaller still, one of them leaving on this day, another on the following day.

7 JESUS THE INEFFECTUAL

WE don't know how much time Jesus and his companions spent in this wandering journey with its minimum of publicity. They passed through the southern part of Galilee, then turned and went up through Tyre and Sidon, returning at length once more to the area near the lake, and Mark's Gospel further suggests, however vaguely, that their steps had led them through also the northern reaches of the Transjordan. As Stauffer says, relative to this journey, it had none of the spectacular aspects that characterized their earlier travels, but "it was done entirely as though they were in flight." It was a journey in which the crowds no longer pressed about them, and there were no shouts of joy in the towns and villages to welcome their entourage. At times they were soaked by the long autumn rains, and at times they could find no roof for shelter overnight.

Whether the time was long or short, the interior life of Jesus had begun a period of struggle more harrowing than his testing in the wilderness of Judea. We have no way of understanding the nature of his interior distress. Profound mystery pervades the heart of Jesus, too deep for the human mind to fathom.

This much can be said: Even during this period of wretched wandering, Jesus' trust in the God of love wavered not the breadth of a hair. Yes, he appealed to God in cries of anguish, but his faith only grew more profound in virtue of his anguish. Obviously, he continued seeking divine guidance on the best way for him to bear testimony to the presence of the all-loving God, but his own sense of trust in God never suffered in the slightest.

Those unfortunate men and women, beyond his counting, whose lives he had crossed in town after town near the lake, were everywhere he looked, in towns that were choked with human misery. These towns and their inhabitants were the whole wide world for him. What could he do, therefore, to make himself the eternal companion of all those unhappy people? In order to reveal to them the love of God he would have to draw them away from their world of forlorn hopelessness. Jesus knew that poverty and disease in themselves are not the hardest things for people to bear; the hardest to bear are the loneliness and the hopelessness that come with being sick or being poor.

Jesus could not accomplish all the miracles the crowds pleaded for. In the towns by the lake he sat to wipe the sweat from a fever-wracked patient whom others had abandoned, and through the night he quietly held the hand of a mother who had lost her child, but miracles he could not do. That is why eventually the crowds called him a "do-nothing" and demanded that he get away from the lake country. Yet the greatest misfortune that Jesus found in the stricken people was their having no one to love them. At the center of all their unhappiness was the wretchedness, fouled with their own hopelessness and loneliness, for want of being loved. What they needed more than miraculous cures was love. Jesus knew the longing of human beings for changeless, enduring companionship. They needed a companion, the kind of a mother who could share their wretched suffering and weep together with them. He believed that God by his nature was not in the image of a stern father, but was more like a mother who shares the suffering of her children and weeps with them; and in order to bear witness to the love which God bore for these men and women in their misfortunes, whenever Jesus met them near the Lake of Galilee he prayed that in God's kingdom they would arrive at his way of seeing things:

Blessed are the poor in spirit,
    for theirs is the kingdom of heaven.
Blessed are those who mourn,
    for they shall be comforted.

Yet how could he himself become the eternal companion of men and women? This was one of the prayers of Jesus in the time of his circuitous journey, while he and his exhausted disciples dragged their feet along the road. It may be that from this very time he began little by little to hear the voice of the loving God coming in answer to him.

Yet still another unlooked-for peril began to pursue them in this trying journey. According to the Gospel of Mark, the members of the surveillance team joined the supporters of Herod Antipas in a plot to assassinate Jesus. Sensing their personal danger, Jesus and the disciples had to stay clear of the realm of Herod. Quietly Jesus said: "I must be on my way today and tomorrow and the next day" (Luke 13:33).

I must be on my way today and tomorrow and the next day. Perhaps it was the great Day of Atonement in the year 30 A.D. when eventually Jesus and his party straggled into the hill country close to Caesarea Philippi, the city built by King Herod Philip to honor the Roman emperor Augustus. Completely surrounded by lofty hills and standing at the headwater of the Jordan River, the city had previously borne the name Baalgad (Joshua 11:17), and also Baal-Hermon (Judges 3:3) because from the crest of the hills one could sight the snow-capped summit of Mount Hermon.

Having arrived in this hill district with his disciples, weary in their fading hopes, Jesus spoke privately to them for the first time concerning the destiny that awaited him. He spoke of his decision to choose them for carrying on in his place. The Gospel of Mark records it in these words:

And he went up into the hills and called to him those disciples whom he desired. And he appointed twelve, to be sent out to preach (Mark 3:13-14).

In general, commentators on the Bible have followed a tradition of fixing the time of Jesus' choosing the twelve apostles near the

beginning of his preaching by the Lake of Galilee. My own opinion is
that the choosing of these disciples took place in the hill country of
Caesarea Philippi, the place to which the group eventually stumbled
their way at the end of the painful and meandering journey that
followed Jesus' expulsion from the lake region and his rejection in his
home town of Nazareth. It is more natural to picture Jesus for the first
time confiding his secret to others, and doing it exclusively for this
handful of men, urging them to pull together in a special bond of
union, but doing so only at a time after these particular men had
stayed close to him in spite of so many others of the group who had
fallen away. We see their wandering journey as a kind of winnowing
process, a chance to test the bond between the disciples and Jesus,
and only after those disciples who were going to leave had finally left
did Jesus entertain hope for the ones who were able to stay. In my
estimation, the passage in chapter 3 of Mark's Gospel (verses 13 to
19) should be attached directly to chapter 8, verse 27. Likewise
Matthew 10:1-14 should be aligned with 16:13, and Luke 6:12-16
with 9:18.

The hills around Caesarea Philippi offer a bird's-eye view of the
town, which is down in the valley. Not far from the town is a spring
from which a tiny brook tumbles in a waterfall. This marks the head of
the Jordan River, and from this source the stream twists and turns a
course to its point of entry into the Lake of Galilee (from where Jesus
and the disciples had begun their own wandering course); then the
river flows out of the lake and runs on down to the wilderness of
Judea. It was in this river, as the disciples knew, that Jesus had
received his baptism at the hand of John the Baptist.

In the course of reminiscing about that earlier day, Jesus told
them: "But then, I have yet to undergo a baptism, and oh, in what an
agony I am till it is accomplished!"

The disciples did not understand Jesus' cryptic reference to
"having yet to undergo a baptism." They could only stare at him—
and see in Jesus a face more wearied than their own, his two eyes
sadder than their own.

"To throw a firebrand upon the earth—that is my mission. And,
oh, how I wish it were already in a blaze!"

The disciples did not yet grasp that for the first time their master
was confiding in them about his approaching death. They did not yet

understand that the whole purpose to his life was to assert the presence of God's love in the real world—and to set this world ablaze with love

Why did Jesus choose such veiled expressions to reveal his passion and death to the disciples? Was he not acting, perhaps, like a mother who has contracted some fatal disease and chooses to intimate to her children her readiness to go, but in words that still will not alarm her children?

Presently Jesus did say it, quietly and openly: "The Son of Man is going the way appointed for him in the Scriptures."

The disciples finally caught up with the master's way of telling them that his destiny was precisely what the prophets had foretold. The prophets? Which of the prophets? The Gospels don't say it, but no doubt the disciples asked him to identify the prophet, and the name of Isaiah then came from the lips of Jesus. He asked them to recall Isaiah's canticle of the suffering servant:

> He was despised, the lowest of men:
> a man of pains, familiar with disease,
> One from whom men avert their gaze—
> despised, and we reckoned him as nothing.

> But it was our diseases that he bore,
> our pains that he carried,
> While we counted him as one stricken,
> touched by God with affliction.

> He was wounded for our rebellions,
> crushed for our transgressions;
> The chastisement that reconciled us fell upon him,
> and we were healed by his bruises.

> All of us strayed like sheep,
> each man turned to his own way;
> And Yahweh brought the transgressions of all of us
> to meet upon him.

> Oppressed he was, and afflicted,
> but he did not open his mouth;
> He was led like a sheep to slaughter;

and as a ewe is speechless before her shearers,
   he did not open his mouth.

By a perverted judgment he was taken away;
   and who was concerned with his case?
For he was cut off from the land of life;
   for our rebellions he was struck dead.

He was given a tomb with the wicked,
   with the evildoers his sepulcher,
Although he had done no violence,
   and there was no deceit in his mouth.

                         (Isaiah 52) (Anchor Bible)

The disciples were unable to sound the depths to the meaning of Jesus. Isaiah's song of the suffering servant was somehow ominous and frightening to hear. Still less were they willing to accept that it was their own master who faced the unhappy destiny of the suffering servant. It was Jesus predicting his own defeat rather than any victory. Why, they wondered, must Jesus undergo such a passion? What sense did it make? Why should God abandon him? The disciples could not comprehend.

In their desperation, perhaps, they put such questions directly to Jesus. We have no way of knowing if he chose to be silent or to reply. What we do know is how they were left with their confusing problem still unsolved. For had they been able to grasp in full the meaning of Jesus, they would have had no cause to react in the consternation they later showed when this terrible manner of death did indeed overwhelm the Master.

So the disciples could muster no more than startled unease to meet this first attempt of Jesus to confide in them. There are, it is true, certain passages in the New Testament which are based on the faith of the primitive Church and which sound as though the disciples were in fact capable of understanding; yet the Gospels of both Matthew and Mark cannot omit confessing to the shock, the unease, the consternation that befell the disciples.

"At this Peter took him by the arm and began to rebuke him:

'Heaven forbid!' he said. 'No, Lord, this shall never happen to you' "
(Matthew 16:22).

"At this Peter took him by the arm and began to rebuke him"
(Mark 8:32).

The reaction was not confined to Peter. The same emotional
response came from all the disciples present when Jesus thus de-
clared himself. The list of the disciples' names appearing in the New
Testament, as I see it, is not necessarily understood as referring
always exclusively to those individuals who are named, for on some
occasions these personal names seem to represent the entire group of
the disciples, or of a certain number within the group (refer, for
example, to the story of Peter's treachery), and this usage becomes
particularly obvious with the names of Peter and Judas. In the
passages we are now considering, it is safe to say that the feelings
ascribed to Peter pertain to all the disciples. A verse in Matthew
makes it perfectly clear that all of them shared Peter's sentiment:
" . . . and the disciples were greatly distressed" (Matthew 17:23). We
can suppose, of course, in connection with the present occasion, that
Jesus likely had more to say, in order to help his disciples to understand.

"For even the Son of Man did not come to be served but to
serve, and to surrender his life as a ransom for many" (Mark 10:45).

"There is no greater love than this, that a man should lay down
his life for his friends" (John 15:30).

We can suppose that also on the present occasion Jesus spoke
such words as these to explain the decision he had announced.
Whenever he uses words like "for many" or "his friends," we
presume that he has in mind not the self-complacent people, like
many of the priests and the doctors of the Law who lived in Tiberias,
but rather the needy men and women near the Lake of Galilee who
came crawling to him from their wretched hovels. He is thinking
about the group of lepers banished from the towns and put away to
fend for themselves in some lonely gully, while never forgetting the
many others he has met—mothers bereaved of their children, old
folks with failing eyesight, a man who couldn't use his legs, a little girl
hovering between life and death. He was there sharing their suffering
with them, carrying their burden with them, becoming an eternal

companion for them. That is why he desired to take all their pains upon himself and be slaughtered, like the Passover lamb of sacrifice. No love is greater than laying down one's own life for one's friends—giving one's life for all mankind. Even if to some this sacrifice seems to be weakness, it still remains the most sublime of attestations to God's existence.

The Gospel of Mark proceeds to record how Jesus commanded the disciples to separate from himself and to go on a mission of preaching. "He then went up into the hill country . . . and appointed twelve as his companions, whom he would send out to proclaim the Gospel" (Mark 3:13-14).

Luke adds that, immediately prior to this action, Jesus spent the whole day in prayer. Very likely this day of prayer was an anguished struggle much like his agony in the garden of Gethsemane, where his prayer became trickling sweat like drops of blood. He felt that his desire was conformed to the will of God—his desire to take upon himself the pain of all mankind in order to become the eternal companion of all.

Jesus decided in the hill country at Caesarea Philippi to separate for a while from his disciples. The separation was by way of preparing the disciples to inherit his own inspiration after his death. It was training not only for missionary work, but also for bearing the hardships which they would in turn be exposed to after his death.

Jesus laid down the following instructions for their journey: (1) travel in groups of two (Ecclesiastes 4:9-10); (2) carry no provisions, no baggage, no money, but simply take a staff, a pair of sandals, and a single tunic (Matthew says they were not to have even the sandals or the staff, and Luke says they were not to take the staff; I have chosen to follow the text of Mark); (3) tell people, "The kingdom of God is at hand"; (4) stay overnight with anyone friendly enough to offer hospitality, but do not impose yourselves on unfriendly people.

"Love your enemies; do good to those who hate you; bless those who curse you; pray for those who treat you spitefully.When a man hits you on the cheek, offer him the other cheek too; when a man takes your coat, let him have your shirt as well. Treat others as you would like them to treat you. . . . Pass no judgment on others. Leave off seeking retribution. Forgive. . . . Be generous. . . ."

I don't know how the disciples took to these practical rules for their journey, but it was around this time also that Jesus taught them that when they prayed, they were to say:

Father, thy name be hallowed;
thy kingdom come.
Give us each day our daily bread.
And forgive us our sins.
For we too forgive all who have done us wrong.

As I mentioned before, I find it impossible to agree with Schweitzer and other commentators who place the time of this apostolic journey in the period of Jesus' ministry near the Lake of Galilee. Nor do I believe that Jesus expected the disciples to return to him crowned with success in their mission of preaching. He knew how their attitude was hardly changed from the time when they despised "the blind beggar" crying out to Jesus and tried to silence him (Mark 10:48), or when they forbade the little children to come to him (Mark 10:13). His real interest was twofold. First, he considered their separation and their journey necessary to prepare them for solid faith on the day when they finally woke up, and for all time after his death. Second, he wanted people outside the confines of Galilee to know that his approaching death was the advent of the "kingdom of God," a universe of love based on the presence of a companion to all mankind. Jesus got the idea of sending the disciples on this mission only after he had sensed the approach of his own death.

The name of Schweitzer has been mentioned, and I might add that this well-known student of the Bible attached great importance to the passage where at Caesarea Philippi Jesus declares for the first time that he himself is "the Messiah":

And Jesus went on with his disciples, to the villages of Caesarea Philippi; and on the way he asked his disciples . . . "And you, who do you say that I am?" Peter answered him, "You are the Christ." And he charged them to tell no one about him.

I repeat what I have already said many times over, that Jesus prior to this time had spoken nothing concerning himself. The word "Christ" is a literal translation for "Messiah," but Jesus had clearly rejected that title, even on the occasion when the common people

near the Lake of Galilee had tried to declare him the "Messiah" —
namely the leader of their nationalist movement.

When at Caesarea Philippi he first broached the question of his
own identity, and Peter replied, "You are the Christ [Messiah]," what
then are we to make of the fact that Jesus apparently confirmed the
title?

A number of present-day scholars consider the whole scene of
this messianic declaration to be a piece of creative writing that springs
from the faith of the early Church. Bornkamm, for example, says:
"This story is woven in its entirety from the confession of faith and
from the ideals of the Church coming some time later. It is not an
historical event that really occurred. The passage may well be a
high-powered historical testimonial to a view of the life of Jesus from
the vantage point of the cross and the resurrection."

Yet neither Bornkamm nor we ourselves can find any material
evidence to support this negative opinion. Even if we are bold
enough to concede that Jesus did not shake his head in disapproval
of Peter's saying "You are the Christ," the incontrovertible fact
remains that a basic difference existed between the "messiah" in
Peter's mind and the "Messiah" in the thinking of Jesus. Peter was
thinking "messiah" in terms of a leader for the nationalist movement,
or a messiah who would expel the foreign conqueror from the land of
Judah, whereas Jesus meant the Messiah of love who would be the
eternal companion of mankind everywhere. I am of the opinion that
the words spoken by Zahrnt in his *Quest for the Historical Jesus* are
right on target: "Jesus never set his own glory as the aim of his
religious teaching. Jesus never demanded a title of honor of any kind
for himself, nor did he ever make his own personality the object of his
preaching."

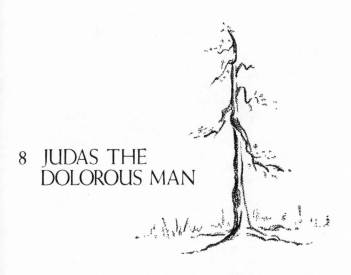

8 JUDAS THE DOLOROUS MAN

We know very little about the activities of Jesus in the next period of his career. The Gospel of John has almost nothing about it and Matthew omits almost everything. Luke contains only a vague reference to Jesus' paying a visit to Samaria.

All of this supports the theory that the temporary separation of Jesus and the disciples, related in the preceding chapter, did not occur near the Lake of Galilee but was closely connected with their wandering journey which followed on the lost hopes for the ministry in Galilee. I mean that once the disciples paired off to go in various directions on the training experiment commanded by Jesus, they could not be eye witnesses to where Jesus stayed and to what he was doing, and so the Gospel authors in turn had no material with which to flesh out their accounts of this particular period.

In any event, we can venture a guess that for this interval Jesus chose to live somewhere in retreat, unknown to others, in order to avoid further misunderstandings concerning himself. He devoted himself to fervent prayer in solitude, and while making his own remote preparation for the passion and death that were coming, he waited there for his disciples to return.

When did they get back, and what had they accomplished? On these points the New Testament says nothing.

But a far different event of great moment did occur at this time in the city of Rome where the man named Sejanus, the holder of enormous political power, had an unfortunate falling out with the emperor Tiberius, which led to his being arrested and put to death. This political shake-up had its profound effect on Pilate, the Roman governor of Judea, and on the Jewish Sanhedrin as well. Pilate, after all, had obtained his position of authority by the patronage of Sejanus, and the Sanhedrin, too, with the shift in power, had reason to fear being divested of the authority which it was holding from Rome. It goes without saying that King Herod Antipas also fell victim to this feeling of insecurity. The heartfelt desire of these three parties was that no political disturbance break out in Judea. They were all on the hot seat at the approach of Passover, the annual festival that always stirred the patriotic spirit of the Jews and they hoped that the festival could end without incident.

The high priest of the temple and presiding officer in the Sanhedrin was Caiaphas, whose basic maxim had always been: Let's not rock the boat. His policy favored peace at any price, not only in politics, foreign and domestic, but in the religious sphere as well. But the policy stood on shaky ground. As I have indicated several times, the soul of the Jewish nation was obsessed with hatred toward the Romans for having conquered their land. No one could predict just when insurrection or revolution might break out were the volatile nation ever to find its spark. Neither the Essenes nor the Pharisees bore any hard feelings against the Zealots, the party of the anti-Roman extremists. And although the Pharisees and the priestly nobility (led by Caiaphas) heartily despised each other, outwardly they maintained their rule only by coalition.

Caiaphas was always in a dilemma. He could not defy the anti-Roman sentiments of his own countrymen, but at the same time he had to preserve the political power of the Sanhedrin which depended on willingness to collaborate with the hegemony of imperial Rome.

It was precisely at this time that the political shake-up occurred in Rome with the execution of Sejanus. If the shock waves ever reached Judea, then Caiaphas and the Sadducees and the entire Sanhedrin could be ousted. And in these unsettled conditions the festival of Passover was drawing near.

As cited earlier we do not know just where it was that Jesus stayed after separating from the disciples, or where he joined them again. But the Sanhedrin was still fearful that in the unsettled political situation somewhere or other the common people might attempt to make Jesus their leader, as had happened earlier near the Lake of Galilee. Their apprehensions were not confined to Jesus alone, but included several other self-proclaimed prophets. The Sanhedrin could not afford to dismiss entirely their misgivings concerning Jesus, even though they were apprised that up in Galilee he was by then considered to be a "do-nothing."

By way of setting background for our later consideration of the judicial proceedings against Jesus, at this point I wish to take a preliminary look at what the Jewish establishment feared most— namely heretics who opposed the Torah— and how these heretics were handled.

1. Whoever insults or in any manner desecrates the temple is worthy of death (Jeremiah 7:10ff.).
2. Whoever claims for self the glory owed to God alone, or who arrogates any prerogative of God, is a blasphemer.
3. Anybody convicted of blaspheming God is to be stoned to death (Leviticus 24:14-16).
4. After the blasphemer has been stoned to death, the corpse shall be strung on a cross-shaped gibbet (Deuteronomy 21:22).
5. Anyone who deliberately violates the sabbath or any other precept of the Law is in contempt of God by reason of his action.
6. If the culprit fails to heed a warning, and continues to violate the Law, he shall be condemned and put to death by stoning.

The above-mentioned laws regarding heterodoxy cover any challenge to God or shirking of the Law or blasphemy. In the eyes of the Sanhedrin, Jesus deserved death by stoning because he had infringed these six particular precepts.

In addition, Jesus was alleged to be a false prophet, and among the laws relating to false prophets those which the Sanhedrin considered applicable to Jesus were, for example:

1. A false prophet is any apostate preacher who, by way of visions, pseudo-prophesies, wizardry or genuine miracle, entices Israel to deny its faith (Deuteronomy 13:2ff.; Leviticus 19:31; etc.).
2. A false prophet shall be condemned by the council and be put to death in Jerusalem (Deuteronomy 13:5).
3. Execution may be administered by strangling. (According to a tradition referred to by Rabbi Judah, Jesus the Nazarene was put to death by strangulation.)
4. Execution may be done by stoning.

His enemies considered Jesus not only a false prophet but also an apostate, and certain other articles in Jewish law pertaining to heterodoxy were considered applicable to the renegade Jesus:

1. Should anybody be under suspicion of apostasy, investigation shall be made into the circumstances of the culprit's birth. The reason is that a bastard child (*mamzer*)—the offspring of an invalid marriage or of illicit intercourse—has a natural bent for treason and for blaspheming God (Leviticus 24:10ff.). (Consideration of these laws adds spice to the canard about Jesus being the illegitimate child of a union between Mary and a Roman soldier.)
2. So long as a bastard lives in conformity with the will of God, he shall not be affronted concerning his origin; but should he turn renegade, his illegitimate birth shall be mercilessly publicized (Leviticus 24:10ff.).
3. The insult of calling one a glutton or a drunkard carries the innuendo of illegitimate birth (Leviticus 21:20). (In the Gospel of John the Pharisees refer to Jesus as a glutton and a heavy drinker.)

Regarding the capital punishment of apostates, the regulations considered applicable to Jesus were the following:

1. The execution of even an innocent person may contribute to the preservation of law and order and to the welfare of God's people.
2. Putting to death an unbeliever benefits both the miscreant and the general public.

3. The execution of apostates shall be carried out with all possible public notice (Leviticus 24:14).
4. Accordingly, executions shall be performed in the seasons of the great pilgrimage festivals (Booths, Passover, and Pentecost), the most opportune moment being when the pilgrims have all assembled in Jerusalem, immediately before the week-long festival, i.e., on the day preceding the great feast day itself.

We find passages in the Bible which incline one to think that Jesus made still another appearance in Jerusalem (John 7:10; Luke 21:37), but we cannot be certain whether or not it happened just at this time. Jesus (in my opinion), anticipating that his passion awaited him in Jerusalem, chose not to move toward the holy city until shortly before the feast of Passover.

In any event, he did rendezvous somewhere or other with the disciples who had been on their training mission. If I dare use my imagination, I picture their meeting place being in the wilderness of Judea, somewhere by the Jordan River, near the spot where he had been baptized by John. At that earlier time he had received his "baptism of water," but now (in his own words) he was about to face the "baptism of his death."

It was the season for the droves of Passover pilgrims heading for the temple in Jerusalem to come pouring from the Jordan Valley and overrun the town of Jericho.

I have mentioned several times that the festival of Passover was characterized by the most intense surge of Jewish nationalistic fervor. It was a definite part of the Jew's religious faith that the Messiah would appear during a Passover and would immediately move to establish the kingdom of Israel. Already adrift in the land was the news about Sejanus being put to death in Rome, and in this year even more than other years the people were fired with yearning for their Messiah to appear.

It so happens that a fellow named Barabbas, with his gang, had just then touched off an anti-Roman uprising. This outbreak was promptly squelched by the Roman military, Barabbas himself being captured and packed off to Jerusalem. The incident served only to fan still higher the flames of anti-Roman sentiment among the pilgrims in the Jordan Valley. We have no historical material relevant to the character of the man Barabbas or to the nature of his uprising.

Scholars have discovered, based on manuscript research in the Gospel of Matthew, that the man whom Pilate finally released in exchange for Jesus also bore the name of Jesus, thus giving rise to the interpretation that this Jesus Barabbas was identical with Jesus of Nazareth, but there is still no conclusive evidence. Other scholars surmise that the uprising of Barabbas might be identified with the insurrection of the Galileans mentioned in Luke 13:1, or again it might be identical with the "incident in the temple treasury" which appears in the *Jewish Antiquities* of Flavius Josephus (18:6-62). But it would be rash to speculate beyond the known and unadorned fact that there did occur some kind of anti-Roman insurrection by Barabbas and his gang.

The incident of Barabbas had stirred its own excitement among the pilgrims crowding into the Jordan River basin near the wilderness of Judea. People were crying "Save Barabbas! Save Barabbas!" and looking for someone to assume the initiative during Passover.

It is against this background that we must consider the atmosphere into which Jesus moved when he appeared once more on the banks of the Jordan, reunited with his disciples. Still alive in the Jordan Valley was the memory of Jesus, the one who after being baptized in the river had become John the Baptist's most promising disciple. People fastened their attention on him when he entered the scene once more. They revived his image as a John the Baptist come to life again. The frenzied pilgrims began to swarm around him.

"Jesus . . . entered the region of Judea beyond the Jordan, and large crowds followed him" (Matthew 19:1).

"So many thousands of the multitude had gathered together that they trod upon one another" (Luke 12:1).

These descriptions from the Gospel record how the people pressed near to Jesus at the Lake of Galilee, prior to Passover in the previous year. Once again, if you will, all was as it had been. Once again, as in the previous year, the pilgrims, each one investing his dreams in Jesus, began to think of making him the leader of his people.

As for the Sanhedrin, this unsettling news reached their ears in Jerusalem without delay. Then the vigilantes swooped down from the holy city to the scene of action. Again they challenged Jesus to debate (Mark 10:1ff.) as they had done the year before, frantic to find anything in his speech to serve as a pretext for arresting him (Luke 11:54). The Sanhedrin, meanwhile, lost no time in opening an emergency session.

> The chief priests and the Pharisees gathered the council and said, ". . . if we let him go on thus, everyone will believe in him, and the Romans will come and destroy both our place and our nation." But Caiaphas said to them, "You know nothing at all. It is expedient for you that one man should die for the people, and that the whole nation should not perish."

Reading this passage, we can understand how extraordinarily fearful the high priest and the Sanhedrin were that the frenzy of the pilgrims down in the Jordan River basin, focusing itself on Jesus, might develop into insurrection, whereupon the Roman authorities would adopt a policy of total suppression of the Jews. At the same time we can surmise why it was that Caiaphas the high priest could think it more prudent to kill off Jesus even if Jesus himself proved to have no intention whatever of becoming the temporal leader of the nation. By killing Jesus, he reasoned, he and his colleagues could ride out the dangerous situation they faced, and by way of conclusion he proposed making Jesus the sacrificial goat.

We don't know whether or not his conclusion received the Sanhedrin's immediate endorsement, but the story undoubtedly reached Jesus and the disciples. According to John's Gospel, Jesus stood in danger of his life from then on.

"So from that day on they took counsel how to put him to death. Jesus, therefore, no longer went openly among the Jews, but went from there to the country near the wilderness, to a town called Ephraim; and there he stayed with the disciples" (John 11:54).

This brief passage implies that the watchdogs dispatched to the Jordan basin had a plan to assassinate Jesus, who in turn avoided any trouble by staying out of the way in the town of Ephraim. Jesus was not changing his own fixed purpose regarding his passion. He was resolved simply not to succumb prior to the Passover festival.

Ephraim is a town of Samaria, the district through which he had previously passed on his return to Galilee following the feast of Booths. In contrast to that occasion, it isn't necessary to suppose that again the Samaritans welcomed the group. But at least the long arm of the inquisitors could not reach him in a town of the Samaritans, who hated all Jews. Jesus and his party were safe for the day of Passover.

At Ephraim, Jesus gave himself to prayer in preparation for the death that was approaching at last. As for the disciples, they were still excited over the enthusiasm for Jesus which swept through the pilgrims in the Jordan Valley. Such a burst of popularity was beyond their expectations, dimmed as they were by the Galilean reverse of the year before. Vanished was the memory of their long and difficult meanderings that ended in Caesarea Philippi; vanished was the memory of all their companions who had fallen away. They felt their hope come alive again. Their attitude comes across bullish in the scene where Jesus and his party are refused hospitality on arriving in Ephraim, when James and John say to Jesus: "Lord, do you want us to order fire to drop from the sky and consume them?" (Luke 9:52ff.). The disciples, even after their training mission, still failed to understand the solitary role of their master, his struggle, and his inner heart.

There emerges now in the disciples' group the face of one individual—the face of the character who fascinates us most—the sullen face of Judas Iscariot, the one who eventually will betray the master.

The materials in the Gospels that deal with Judas Iscariot are unfortunately all too scanty. Later I intend to present the dramatic scene where Judas betrays Jesus. For the moment I shall give no more than a simple account of his origin and his career.

His place of birth is a mystery to the scholars. Cheyne says that the word "Iscariot" is a variant of Jericho, the name of the world's oldest city, in the wilderness of Judea. Others say that the surname bears no connection with his birthplace, but that "Iscariot" relates in meaning to the Latin word *sicarius*, i.e., "dagger man," in which case the meaning was extended to include the idea of "assassin," and from there the scholars are free to speculate about Judas being one of the anti-Roman terrorists.

We know nothing about the man's personal history. By supposing that "Iscariot" was a local corruption of the Latin word *scortia* ("leather tunic"), one scholar states flatly that Judas followed the trade of a leather worker, but there is no way in the world to verify that opinion.

So be it. We have no evidence relating to his place of birth or to his personal history, yet I have the feeling that among the disciples, exuberant in those days immediately before the feast of Passover, the only one to stay cold sober was Judas. During those days when the others began once more to think of Jesus becoming the nation's leader, it was Judas alone who knew in his heart that Jesus would reject the whole idea. In that sense he was the only one of the disciples to show an odd understanding of Jesus.

On a day shortly before the arrival of Passover, Jesus suddenly announced to the group that he would depart from Ephraim, cut across the wilderness of Judea, and go up again to Jerusalem by way of Jericho.

"Rabbi, only recently the Jews wanted to stone you to death, and you mean to go back there again?"

Jesus shook his head.

"Lazarus, our friend, has fallen asleep. Well, then, I will go and wake him from his sleep."

From this place in the text begins the famous miracle story about the resurrection of Lazarus, but we are free to think that "Lazarus" symbolizes the dead, namely the Jews who were as yet unaware of the God of love. Such people were next to being dead, and he must rouse them from their sleep by means of his own death.

Again the disciples mistook his meaning. They interpreted the master's talk about "waking from sleep" as a sign that he himself was ready to make a stand. The languid lion had finally found its legs. They thought he was now agreed that the time was ripe to accept the expectations of the people. The disciple named Thomas, in a burst of excitement, cried out to the others: "Let us also go, that we may die with him" (John 11:16).

Those were words from a disciple who understood nothing—the zeal of a disciple who could not fathom Jesus. How painful that was for Jesus himself! Thanks to the words of Thomas, Jesus again was made to realize how he himself would be all alone till the moment he died.

Leaving Samaria, Jesus went east toward the Jordan Valley.

Like other pilgrims going to Jerusalem he turned south on reaching the valley and moved toward the town of Jericho. With his premonitions of the passion, "Jesus was walking ahead of them" (Mark 10:23). This sentence expresses a detail which the eyewitness disciples long afterward must have talked about repeatedly. It makes us visualize clearly the isolated figure of Jesus.

Eventually all the pilgrims on their way to Jerusalem crowded into one another where the Jordan River enters the dun-brown wilderness of Judea. Their voices rose in a yell of welcome to Jesus. From across the wilderness they were already in sight of the elevated parapets of Jericho.

A whirlwind of excitement swept the pilgrims. Together they shouted, "Jesus, Son of David!" (Luke 18:38ff.). The multitude, like the disciples themselves, thought that Jesus had now agreed to their hopes. Hemmed about on every side by masses of people, Jesus quietly spoke for the ears of the disciples only: "Listen! We are going up to Jerusalem, and the Son of Man will be betrayed to the high priests and the scribes" (Mark 10:33). But his softly spoken words were lost in the clamor of the crowd and never reached the disciples, who themselves were mesmerized by the general frenzy.

Jericho was situated, in the time of Jesus, a short distance away from the city we see today. The former place is now so completely in ruins that even a visit to the site yields no idea of the ancient city's plan. Nothing remains of it except a place—remarkable in the wilderness of Judea—where springs of water are flowing in the shade of eucalyptus trees and cedars of Lebanon. Nearby lie the ruins from the palace built by King Herod the Great for his winter resort. The population of the city always exploded on the approach of Passover. The pilgrims going to Jerusalem passed through Jericho.

Jesus spent the night in the home of Zacchaeus, the local chief of the tax collectors, and the next morning an enthusiastic crowd squeezed in around the house (Mark 19:1). He no longer bothered to shake his head to deny the people's frenzied misunderstanding of him. Denial had always been futile, even back in the days when he spoke his true purpose to the same sort of crowds in Galilee.

By that afternoon, Jesus and the disciples were again on the road leading up to Jerusalem through the hills by way of the dry creek beds (wadi). The narrow road threaded a pass between bald mountains supporting not a single tree. The sun was quite severe even for a day in the season of Passover. Most likely Jesus remained silent while he walked the desolate landscape, itself hung over in silence.

After laboriously working their way through the hills, the travelers emerged onto a broad plateau. Eventually they came in sight of a tiny village of whitewashed houses. It was Bethany. Jesus and his companions found lodging that day in the home of a resident by the name of Simon. In Simon's house lived two young women named Mary and Martha. And here the Gospels of Mark and John bring Judas Iscariot to stage center.

Very likely, on reaching Bethany, the fanatics who trailed after Jesus and his party all the way from Jericho crowded around the house of Simon. Their voices overwhelmed the normally quiet village with yells like "Jesus, Son of David! Jesus for Messiah! Jesus for Messiah!" and the shouting could be heard inside the house. Suddenly Mary (more extroverted in character than her homebody older sister) produced a jar of costly perfume oil of spikenard, and lavishly she poured the lotion on the feet of Jesus. Mary's act was more than a gesture of hospitality. She was acting in accord with the shouts that bounced from wall to wall of the other houses: "Jesus, Son of David!" and "Jesus for Messiah! Jesus for Messiah!" In any event, *the root meaning of the word "messiah" is "one who is anointed with oil."*

The disciples naturally caught the intent of Mary's act. It stirred their emotions. Never had there been a gesture of welcome for the master to compare with this one.

But for the moment, Judas was the only one to find his tongue: "Why was not this perfume sold for three hundred denarii and the money given to the poor?"

The sweet fragrance of the ointment filled the entire house (John 12:3), and when all present were visibly touched in their emotions, only the voice of Judas introduced a chilling tone. His manner of speaking was rude, as though he alone possessed any common sense.

Judas recognized as well as anyone else why Mary did what she had done. The author of John's Gospel interprets the outburst of Judas as a piece of hypocrisy. But the words of Judas imply something deeper. Judas is saying it clearly—that Jesus will never become the messiah that everybody seeks.

While the rest of the disciples were no better than the pilgrims in their ignorance of the mind of Jesus, within the group Judas Iscariot alone was aware of the master's secret. Judas however, knowing what he knew, was far from happy with what he knew. For the first time he openly challenges Jesus: "Why was this ointment not sold for three hundred denarii and given to the poor?" The words reveal his feeling that in this visible world what really counts are tangible results: Master, you have preached a love that has no meaning in the real world. Your kind of love does not pay off. You aspire to becoming the eternal companion of all misfortunate people. Yet these misfortunates, would they not themselves prefer to receive the three hundred denarii I speak of?

We cannot think that Judas was only peevishly insubordinate. He was one of the handful who continued to follow the master even when most of the disciples, one after another, were abandoning Jesus. Having persevered as far as he did, always close to Jesus, there must have occurred a painful struggle in the soul of Judas, once he perceived the true intent of Jesus which none of the others had yet been able to grasp. It would seem that Jesus himself gave credence to Judas. He had entrusted Judas with the common purse belonging to the group (John 12:6), a sign that Judas truly had the confidence of Jesus.

Possibly the words spoken by Judas were intended to be his final advice for Jesus: "Master, you have resolved to meet death in order to become the eternal companion of all mankind. The people's demand, however, is different. Isn't it true that up there in Galilee, too, the lepers didn't hanker for love? Obviously they wanted only to be cured, the cripples wanted only to be able to walk, the blind wanted only to see. That's human nature." It could be that some such idea as this lay behind the recorded words of Judas.

Here is how Jesus replied: "I did not allow Mary's lavishing the fragrant ointment on me with the idea of my being the earthly messiah. I allowed it because what she has done will turn out to be preparation for my burial" (John 12:7).

On this occasion again, he denied being a *messiah* in the meaning that everyone clamored for. He was also unmistakably telling

Judas that his own resolve to die remained without change.

Judas alone was capable of getting the point of the master's reply. He alone sensed how there was to be no switch in the master's destiny. What is more, Judas even imagined to himself how his fellow disciples would all abandon Jesus when the time would come. For the moment, however, Judas was the only one to conceive that Jesus might be arrested, might be tortured, might die, alone.

9 "JERUSALEM! JERUSALEM!"

WE finally turn the page of the book to Act Three, the most dramatic part of the Gospel story. This third act is the climax to the entire Bible, and for a scribbler of novels like me in Japan this particular drama never grows stale, no matter how many times I read it. I never get away from my opinion that the scenes in the passion and death of Jesus, portrayed in the Gospels, are more effective by far than most of the classic tragedies in the history of literature. Tragedy always portrays the passion and death of heroes, but this biblical Third Act portrays the death of more than merely a human hero. No other tragic drama introduces to the stage a sacred aureole to match the halo which radiates from the Holy One, and which suddenly we cannot fail to be sensible of as the aureole plays its course against the grizzly backdrop to the dramatic action. Not only that, but everyone's questions regarding Jesus, hitherto played as so many underplots, are brought to center stage in the characters surrounding Jesus in this third act—those who betray Jesus and those who condemn Jesus—all brought to ineluctible confrontation with their own specific problems and with the riddle of Jesus himself. Not only Jesus, but each one of the characters on stage is a vibrant human being even more so than in other Gospel scenes, and we can visualize their every gesture and every change of facial expression. We can discover even among ourselves characters like Peter and Judas or the other disciples, all of whom betrayed Jesus, or the likes of the high priests Annas and Caiaphas, who condemned him, or of the centurion (platoon commander) who escorted him to the place of execution, or simply the likes of those in the crowd who jeered and threw stones at him.

In reading Act Three—all the scenes are usually referred to collectively as the passion narrative—we are impelled to question how far the descriptions represent actual fact—whether to some extent they have not been retouched by the early Christian Church, or, at least for a few of the scenes, whether they are not completely fabricated. For example, a certain legend emanating from those Jews who sat in judgment of Jesus relates that he was not crucified but was put to death in some other way. Of course I am cognizant of the earliest professional historian to mention Jesus—the Jew Flavius Josephus, whose *Jewish Antiquities* attests that "he was condemned to be crucified"—although most historians believe that this particular passage is not from the hand of Flavius himself but is an interpolation made by Christians in a later century.

What is more, if we compare the passion narrative with certain pages in the Old Testament, we will often discover striking similarities of scene. Look, for example, at the twenty-first chapter of Matthew (verses 1-11) where Jesus, seated on a burro, enters Jerusalem in a triumph of welcoming cheers from the crowds (Mark 11:1-10; Luke 19:29-44). "The disciples went and did as Jesus had directed them; they brought the ass and colt, and put their garments on them, and he sat thereon. . . . "

For anybody who has done some reading in the Old Testament, this scene will bring to mind an oracle in the ninth chapter of the Book of Zechariah:

Rejoice greatly, O daughter of Zion!
  Shout aloud, O daughter of Jerusalem!
Lo, your king comes to you:
  triumphant and victorious is he,
Humble and riding on an ass,
  on a colt the foal of an ass.

The same chapter in Matthew, after quoting the italicized words to describe how Jesus entered Jerusalem seated on the ass' colt, continues immediately:

> The crowds that went before him [Jesus on the burro] and that followed him shouted, "Hosanna to the Son of David! Blessed is he who comes in the name of the Lord! Hosanna in the highest!"

Anyone comparing these two passages will be struck by the fact that the two descriptions are substantially the same. Then it becomes impossible to deny categorically any interpretation of Jesus on the burro which holds that this scene does not represent any actually occurring historical fact in the final journey of Jesus to Jerusalem— but that when the story of the passion, as told by the disciples, was eventually redacted for inclusion in the liturgy of the early Christian Church, this passage as it now appears in Matthew was in fact composed from the ninth verse of the ninth chapter in the Book of Zechariah.

Carrying this point of view still further, as for example Bornkamm does in his famous book *Jesus of Nazareth*, it is clear that the description of the betrayal by Judas, which is part of the Last Supper, is actually drawn from the words of Psalm 41:

> Even my bosom friend in whom I trusted,
>   who ate my bread,
> Has lifted his heel against me. . . .

and also that the price of thirty pieces of silver paid to Judas by the Sanhedrin was lifted directly from the twelfth verse in the eleventh chapter of Zechariah: "And they weighed out thirty shekels of silver [as the price of God]."

But to continue commenting in detail on each and every one of such quotations begins to clutter the thrust of the narrative, so I will cite just a few more scenes from the passion, match them in order with words from the Old Testament, and then put an end to it.

1 Pilate . . . scourged Jesus. . . . And the soldiers struck his head with a reed, and spat upon him. . . . (Mark 15:16-19).

I gave my back to the smiters, and my cheeks to those who pulled out the beard; I hid not my face from shame and spitting (Isaiah 50:6).

2. And when the soldiers had mocked him, they stripped him of the purple cloak, and put his own clothes on him (Mark 15:20).

The divided my garments among them, and for my raiment they cast lots (Psalm 22:18).

3. [When Jesus was arrested] the disciples all forsook him, and fled (Mark 14:50).

"Strike the shepherd, that the sheep may be scattered" (Zechariah 13:7).

It is wrong of course to conclude from parallel passages of this kind that the entire passion narrative is a piece of fiction into which the authors inserted images ignited in their brains by contact with certain words in the Old Testament; and on this point it seems to me that Bornkamm goes to extremes.

At the same time, however, it is perilous to insist that various scenes in the passion narrative represent the historical facts in every detail.

Where the scholars are at odds with one another concerning which passages are factual and which are fictional, I hold to a single constructive attitude. I myself like to draw a clear distinction in meaning between *facts* and *truths* in the Gospels. I am ready to admit that the many scenes woven into the New Testament text do not necessarily represent the hard facts which they profess to depict in the passion narrative. Yet even non-factual scenes can still present truth, because they derive from the faith of people who believed in Jesus. Faith far and away transcends the trivialities of non-essential fact, and because in the depths of their hearts the believers of that generation wished them so, the scenes are therefore true. Quite possibly Jesus never did take his ride on the donkey, but, being resolved to submit to death, he actually chose rather to enter the capital quietly. Yet after the death of Jesus those people who could not forget him adapted his entry into Jerusalem to the words in Zechariah 9:9 to depict a glorious scene that symbolized for them the reality of the Savior Messiah.

Having been eyewitness to the horrible death of Jesus, they had to confront the mystery of why it was that this man, even while he was their Savior, would have to undergo so horrible a death. Their own anguish may have made them create the scene. I'll go so far as to say that this scene represents truth precisely because they could not escape creating it. From my own position as a novelist I wish to say that creative composing is not to be equated with telling a lie.

Granted that certain fictional strands have been woven into the narrative, in no way can they vitiate the true meaning of the passion. The truth is that Jesus, in pursuing his mission, came to a showdown with the Jerusalem Sanhedrin, who dragged him off to Pilate and then to King Herod, and that his love was therefore the reason for his execution. No matter how many parallel passages Bornkamm may cite from the Old Testament, it still remains true that the disciples did betray their master, and that afterward Peter and all of them shed tears for their treachery. The early Church spoke clearly and concretely about the weakness and the treachery of Peter, the head of the Church, and of the other immediate disciples of Jesus, simply because these were the plain facts, impregnable to any overhaul. (Regarding the weakness of Peter himself, of course we can observe, between the time when the Church was first organized and the period of time that followed, a change in the tone of the words employed to describe the plight of Peter, a shift that becomes clear by contrasting Mark with the other Gospels; but the change in itself is insignificant.)

From here on in my analysis of the passion narrative I intend to follow the chronological order of the events. At the same time I will strive to keep in mind always whatever pertains to the various people whom Jesus faced. What was the position of the Sanhedrin at the moment? What went through the mind of Pilate? What was the role of King Herod? The mob? The disciples?

Jesus spent one night as guest in the home of Simon of Bethany, and on the following day, which was Monday, he finally arrived in Jerusalem.

From the village of Bethany to the city of Jerusalem was scarcely half an hour's walk. Moving from the village and across the Mount of Olives, a twist in the road revealed as if by magic a panoramic view of the dun-brown holy city within its fortified walls. The temple itself resembled a citadel, and immediately behind the temple stood the lofty Antonia Tower. The city walls soared above the valley, high enough to be intimidating, and behind them at some distance stood the palace of King Herod, and south of that the mansion of Caiaphas the high priest. All along the valley and all across the lower slope of Mount Olivet stirred the masses of pilgrims who had come for the Passover festival bringing their domestic animals.

The Gospel of Mark says that Jesus came down from the mountain riding a donkey, and that the pilgrims on catching sight of him began waving palm leaves, while others spread their cloaks on the road and still others cut branches from the trees, and all of them lustily cheered:

Hosanna!
A blessing on him
Who comes in the name of the Lord!
A blessing on our father David's throne,
which is now to be restored!
Hosanna in the heavens above!

Whether this description fits what actually happened, I don't know. As I said, the description may well be a piece of fiction based on the ninth chapter of the Old Testament Book of Zechariah,

Rejoice greatly, O daughter of Zion!
Shout aloud, O daughter of Jerusalem!
Lo, your king comes to you;
triumphant and victorious is he,
Humble and riding on an ass,
on a colt the foal of an ass.

But whether literally true or not, this passage in Mark's Gospel brings home to us the spirit then prevailing in Jerusalem and the excitement of the pilgrims.

Just as in the town of Jericho, the crowds now welcomed Jesus not as a "do-nothing" but as the complete "man of action."

The *Pesach* (Passover) was at hand. The people preparing for the festival were looking back on their long history, rueful over the anguished adversity of their ancient wandering migrations, and they prayed with fervor that God would come again to restore prosperity to his land now trampled underfoot by the Gentiles. Jesus, of course, knew the spirit of the feast. On this particular day, shortly before the festival itself began, with full knowledge he dared to plunge into that whirlpool of popular misunderstanding. Descending from the Mount of Olives and through the cheers from the crowd, he certainly knew that he was soon going to disappoint these people, and that the people in their frustration would then turn against him. C. H. Dodd bluntly confesses to feeling something ominous in the whole procedure. Religious pictures tend to portray the figure of Jesus on this occasion as a triumphant hero. The fact is that Jesus, coming down the mountain and entering the city, wore a painful smile, which came with pondering his own isolation. He recalled how the multitudes around him near the Lake of Galilee were disappointed and disillusioned with him on that day of the Sermon on the Mount, and how they went away in anger and deserted him. Now he would not have long to wait for an even more drastic turn of fortune to present itself, worse than the day of his Sermon on the Mount. He had not long to wait before these pilgrim visitors as well would turn against him. Tomorrow? Would it be perhaps the day after tomorrow? The only thing he was determined on was the day for him to die. It would be the day on which the festival of Passover began, the day when the people made reparation to God for their sins by slaughtering a lamb and bearing it to the temple. On the day the lamb was sacrificed, Jesus too would die, in the same manner.

The Sanhedrin—composed of Sadducees and Pharisees— were naturally aware of his arrival in the city. Not all of them necessarily shared the same reaction, for even within the Sanhedrin certain members actually favored Jesus, especially among the Pharisees, the sect more closely tied to the common levels of society. Obviously discomfited were those in the Sanhedrin who followed the party line of the high priest Caiaphas. They had no way of knowing what it was that motivated Jesus, who had recently retired into Samaria from the wilderness of Judea, to enter Jerusalem itself with no apparent fear for any personal danger.

Immediately they summoned a meeting. What is Jesus up to? Why doesn't he stay out of sight? What shall we do from here on? Back and forth they argued policy, one against the other.

I have related how at a previous emergency meeting Caiaphas the high priest had proposed arresting Jesus. Should they take that action now? Yet for the moment their own position was too weak to warrant direct action. Their problem lay in the unprecedented popular enthusiasm for Jesus, the swelling clamor of support, which had spread from the desert to the town of Jericho and from there to Jerusalem. If they ignored his popularity and took him into custody, they would infuriate the visiting pilgrims, who had the idea that only Jesus could rescue Barabbas, who were coming to the point of thinking that Jesus himself was the messiah.

If the pilgrims should fly into a passion, and if that should lead to open insurrection, the Roman Empire, in the person of Pilate the governor, would lay the responsibility on no one else but Caiaphas the high priest and his council. They could not afford to antagonize the pilgrims. In their position they resorted then to the solution always open to politicians faced with a hard choice. They would watch and wait. They would play for time.

To see the situation in this way explains why the Sanhedrin failed to molest Jesus during the three days from Monday until Thursday, in spite of many opportunities to arrest him. It explains why Jesus was free to appear every day in the temple and speak to the people about the love of God and the God of love (Luke 19:47).

In his audience, of course, the secret agents of the Sanhedrin were always present. They were still out to challenge Jesus in debate, always devising some ploy or other by which they hoped to destroy the people's faith in him.

It was probably on Wednesday, the third day after his arrival in Jerusalem, when Jesus carried out the famous incident called the cleansing of the temple. According to the Gospel of Mark, Jesus personally ordered the hucksters in the temple courtyard to vacate the premises; then he tipped over the tables of the money-changers and the seats of the pigeon venders, telling them all that the temple was a place for prayer.

How are we to interpret this action of Jesus, apparently so out of character? Did the action really happen? Many commentators have varying opinions. Among those recent biblical scholars who see in Jesus an ultra-nationalist political revolutionary, there is one for example who is wild enough to say that this incident in the temple comes to us in a redacted version of "a scheme on the part of Jesus to occupy the temple precincts by using the tactics Barabbas had used in his raid on a Roman army installation in Palestine." But if Jesus ever launched a rebellious act of that kind, the Roman military would have acted quickly to suppress it. Neither the Roman army, however, nor the temple security guards controlled by the Sanhedrin, made any move at the time, a fact which shows this view to be no more than strained imagination.

I think, with Cullman, that the incident rather shows us Jesus taking the offensive to challenge the priests who administered the temple and who gathered in the accruing revenues. There was something greater than the temple, and that something greater was love. It would be appropriate to think that Jesus was this time expressing his thought not in words but in action.

But neither is that the whole explanation. If I may add another idea: Jesus had decided to die at Passover. The Sanhedrin had spent three days at its game of sly temporizing. The feast itself was only two days away. Is it possible that Jesus by his action was inviting his own arrest at their hand? This is, of course, no more than my private speculation. Yet the Sanhedrin never moved a finger. Nor did the temple security guard make any move at the time to apprehend him. That was because the activity of Jesus ironically gained him further support from the visiting pilgrims. They took the action of Jesus as a warning to the Sanhedrin for the way it was compromised with Rome, and they misunderstood it to be a patriotic move toward reform of the Jewish religion.

Jesus knew that his popularity and the people's support, based on widespread misunderstanding, would soon wind up in disaster for him: It will not be long before you will all reject me. It will not be long before you throw your support to those who lay violent hands on me. I will not do what you hope for. It won't be long before I appear to be a "washout" and a "do-nothing." When that happens, you will be angry, you will jeer at me, you will despise me, as Isaiah has foretold.

When evening came and the pilgrims cleared the temple precincts, Jesus also disappeared. We don't know where he lodged, in company with the disciples, during these days. Some think that they spent the nights at Gethsemane, a place for pressing oil from the olive fruit, on the lower part of the Mount of Olives, while others say that they were provided lodging at the home of Simon in Bethany.

We do know the nature of the nighttime hours of Jerusalem in the season of Passover. The heat of the day abruptly chills. When you raise your eyes to the cold night sky, the stars shine big and bright. The visiting pilgrims used to sleep in the open fields, close to the livestock they had brought with them, and all was wrapped in silence. Moonbeams bathed the somber, intimidating city walls, soaring up on the other side of the Kedron Valley. Jesus alone kept watch, thinking of his imminent passion and death. Even so, the disciples noted nothing. Even on the final night, they were fast asleep. How difficult it is, how heartbreaking, this bearing witness to the reality of the God of love! And even though the time for him to bear his witness was close at hand, the disciples are fast asleep. If among them only one, perhaps, could sense the crisis coming near, it was Judas Iscariot.

Judas Iscariot. His motives likely were not quite as simplistic as what is written in the Gospel of John. Were he the owner of a simple mentality, he would have quit the master long before, near the Lake of Galilee, or during the days of those painful wanderings in the north. His failure to break with Jesus would seem to indicate that he shared the other disciples' dream that Jesus would stage a comeback and would then restore the ancient glory of Israel in accord with their hopes. Those scholars who interpret Judas as a rabid patriot with a bent for politics are not necessarily wrong. Judas, however, had felt his dream gradually crumble away since the time when Jesus spoke at Caesarea Philippi. His misgivings were only confirmed by what happened in the Jordan Valley close to the wilderness of Judea, and after that in Jericho. His decisive showdown with Jesus had occurred just three days ago, at the home of Simon in Bethany. But if so, why did he string along with Jesus as far as Jerusalem? Probably not even Judas himself was able to sort out the intricate forces at work in his own hurt psyche. This Jesus with the sunken eyes, looking older than his years: the more wretched Jesus appeared to be, the more he exerted some indescribable fascination for Judas. Like the rest of the handful of disciples who stayed with him until the catastrophe, even Judas felt that if he himself were to desert Jesus, he would be plagued somehow for the rest of his life with unspeakable tension, remorse, and loneliness. He wrestled many times with his own mood. He tried to kill off his own attachment to Jesus. His heart was like the state of the man who has been disillusioned by his woman, yet who, in attempting to separate from her, discovers sadly that he cannot live without her.

Did he continue to think that Jesus yet might change his mind? There were still two days remaining until Passover. Maybe Judas hoped that in these two days Jesus could still change his mind. He loved Jesus as he loved himself, and he hated Jesus as he hated himself. This ambivalent attitude, this brew of love and hatred, made him keep his eyes glued to Jesus from close up after they arrived in Jerusalem.

10 THE NIGHT OF THE ARREST

THE time had finally come. It was Thursday.

John disagrees with the Synoptics in determining the date within the month of Nisan for this particular day of the week. (In terms of the modern calendar, Nisan ran from the middle of March to the middle of April.) The Synoptics imply that Thursday was the 14th of Nisan, while John thinks it was the 13th, but we have no need to choose among the various arguments offered by the experts in support of either side. The point is really irrelevant to the heart of the story.

For this particular day the first event recorded in the Gospels is the famous Last Supper, the final meal together for Jesus and the disciples, a scene often painted by Leonardo da Vinci and other Christian artists.

The day was most likely one of those beautiful clear-sky days that mark the season in that part of the world. But as always on this particular date the confines of the city were choked in dust-raising bustle. Hucksters along the narrow winding streets hawked their wares to passers-by—they offered unleavened bread for the Passover feast, and the bitter herbs, and pigeons. Sheep and donkeys were carried along in the surging streams of humankind. At strategic points in the maze of streets Roman soldiers were "stationed on alert to forestall any riots," according to Josephus. The governor of Judea, Pontius Pilate, was present in the city, moving up from Caesarea on the Mediterranean coast in order to keep an eye on the Passover celebration. Pilate had heard the name of Jesus, but the name had stirred hardly a ripple of interest or concern in him. What did occupy the governor's mind was the recent turn of events back in Rome—the fall from imperial favor of Sejanus, the political boss to whom Pilate was obliged for his own rise to power.

Also present in the Holy City was Herod Antipas, the ruler of Galilee, who stayed in that section referred to in modern times as the palace of Herod, not far from the fortress Antonia, where Pilate was staying (according to André Parrot). The two authorities were locked in a dismal rivalry which kept both of them ever alert to reap the advantage from any political misstep committed by the other. Herod Antipas, too, had entertained reports about Jesus, and in fact he had been rendered more than a little curious on hearing some time back that Jesus was a John the Baptist come to life again. But his curiosity by now had faded away.

The festival lasted eight days, beginning from the eve of the feast of Passover, i.e., from the 14th of Nisan. During the morning of the 14th every Jewish family threw away all of the ordinary bread in the house, and during the week that followed, the people ate only the brittle elongated pieces of unleavened bread called *mazzoth*. In the afternoon they slaughtered the sacrificial lamb. Usually it was the head of the household, or the representative of a group, who brought his lamb up to the temple and killed it there in the temple courtyard. The blood of the lamb was collected and handed to the priests, who in turn poured the blood over the altar of sacrifice.

The flesh of the lamb was then carried home to be served at the festive Passover table. The meal in which Jesus participated, the meal referred to as the Last Supper, is to be identified with this festive board of Passover.

Did Jesus on Thursday go up to the temple area as he had done on each of the three preceding days? And if he did, what happened there? We don't really know. But all day Thursday the temple area was jammed with crowds of men on one another's heels, coming to slaughter their lambs. The broad esplanade of the temple resounded from every direction with the hubbub of bleating sheep mixed with the singsong voices of men at their prayers.

Did Jesus address any message to the people on this particular day as he had done on the three preceding days? It does seem likely that it was on Thursday, or possibly the day before, that he pointed out the temple and said, "You see these great buildings? Not one stone will be left upon another; all will be thrown down." "Destroy this temple, and in three days I will raise it again."

These words of Jesus were interpreted as blasphemy against the temple when the sayings were repeated at his trial on the following day.

Although it is not explicitly said so in the Scriptures, we can easily imagine that on Thursday the mass of pilgrims who had come to the city were keeping their eyes on Jesus as the eve of the great festival drew nearer and nearer. For the past three days they had been awaiting the moment for Jesus to rise to the occasion. The loud bleating of the sheep being slaughtered in the temple, and the maelstrom of people who in the afternoon packed the temple courtyards to the point where not one more could enter until another came out—the frenzy of the scene was bound all the more to whet their messianic hopes. Doubtless every move and every act of Jesus drew the people's curiosity and held their interest.

In its own way the Sanhedrin, too, was geared to react against any contingency.

We must always consider the Thursday evening supper within the context of the entire day as I have described it. The Last Supper becomes more than a group of intimate friends gathering quietly for dinner. Anyone witnessing a Jewish *seder* even once becomes immediately aware that the sacred meal is more than the usual dinner party held to honor some occasion. It is no ordinary family reunion for dinner. At the *seder* the head of the house breaks the unleavened bread; then after a liturgical prayer he explains to his family the deep significance of the feast day. He recalls for them the many sufferings which their forefathers endured in their wandering migrations. Then as he passes around the cup of wine he prays for them to be redeemed from all the humiliations which have been the fate of them and their forefathers.

Superficial reading of the scriptural narratives might leave an impression that the Last Supper was a very quiet gathering in private for Jesus and the few disciples. But is that how it was? In describing an earlier occasion, the Gospels tell how in the town of Jericho the crowd pushed into the house where Jesus was staying, squeezing in where there was standing room for not another soul. Therefore, on this particular Thursday we have no reason to think that the excited pilgrims were not curious to know where Jesus would be eating the Passover meal.

The Synoptic Gospels all record the Last Supper as taking place in a certain house reserved by Jesus for the occasion. The house, located somewhere in Jerusalem, belonged to a man who was a friend of Jesus, a man who, after making all the necessary preparations, was waiting to receive him. We can suppose that quite a crowd of people trailed along while Jesus and the disciples were proceeding to the house. The crowd kept urging him to take advantage of their presence and declare himself their leader. We can imagine how the cheers and the shouts of hope affected the ears of the disciples themselves, and how the excitement whirling about them grew more and more intense.

For this reason I cannot bring myself to accept the atmosphere of the Last Supper or the composition of the scene as depicted in the tradition of the master painters of the West. Not only the artists, but most of the world's Christians as well, influenced by the account in John's Gospel, imagine for themselves a three-sided arrangement around a table, Jesus being seated in the middle, with Peter to the right and John to the left, Judas Iscariot next to John, and so on for the Twelve.

In modern times a tourist to Jerusalem is guided to an ancient building called the House of the Last Supper. The building, showing stars and lions executed in relief, stands close to a mausoleum known as David's Tomb. A cenacle preserved within the house clearly coincides in all detail with the traditional popular fancy. Yet, to be honest, both the house itself and its cenacle are humbug, and, falling in line with the humbug, the generations of master painters never did get around to depicting the atmosphere of the Last Supper as it was in life. I think it most likely that genuine local coloring for the Last Supper would include a crowd of people pressing about the house, with the boldest souls from among them pushing into the dining room itself to listen with the disciples to the words of Jesus.

The more important point, however, lies elsewhere. Putting together the two ideas of "a meal" and "a crowd" leads the memory by its laws of association to recall another and previous event. The scene of the Last Supper links unmistakably with that other scene near the Lake of Galilee—again a day close to Passover— when Jesus freely provided a meal for the crowd that pressed about him. I have already discussed what lay at the heart of that earlier scene—how Jesus shook his head to deny the messianic hopes focused on him by the crowd assembled on the mountainside. The Sermon on the Mount clearly showed that the God of love whom he preached bore no resemblance whatsoever to the image of any chauvinistic, temporal messiah. As a result of that sermon people became disillusioned. They fell away from Jesus and went to the other extreme of driving him off.

The Last Supper now repeats what happened with the Sermon on the Mount. The turn of events for these two occasions are described almost in parallel. I wish to draw attention to how the Gospel account of the Last Supper itself recreates the circumstances of that other event the year before near the Lake of Galilee.

The form-critics (following Bultmann) deny the historicity of the Last Supper, supposing the narrative to be a literary creation born of Christian liturgical traditions, or they suppose that it originated with the Hellenized Church under the influence of Paul. Bornkamm goes so far as to say that "from the biblical text itself we cannot today discover for certain just how the Last Supper was carried out, because our present text reflects the eucharistic celebration and other liturgical practices of the later Church." On the other hand these experts have no comment whatsoever concerning the general state of excitement among the pilgrim visitors and the passionate susceptibilities of the crowd on the evening of the supper.

I myself take the Last Supper to be an historical event, even though I do not go along with the tradition of limiting the scene only to Jesus and the Twelve clinging together in hushed and solemn comportment. Rather I imagine a dramatic scene that bristles with a

twofold confrontation, between Jesus and the pilgrims, and between Jesus and the disciples.

As I mentioned earlier, in the few days since Jesus came up to
Jerusalem, he had settled in his own mind that the time had come
for a final break with the crowd of pilgrims and other people clinging
about him. The Messiah of love he most certainly was, but he had
no ambition whatsoever to be the political messiah of people's expectations. He had strongly pleaded his case to be accepted as the
eternal companion of all men, but he had no thought of becoming
the earthly leader craved by the masses. Hence he thought the time
had come to break with the crowd, to break with all the people who
supported him for the wrong reason. The supper would be his final
contact; that was the main motif of the Last Supper.

The Gospels develop this motif with four variations. First is the
passage where Jesus institutes the mystery of the Eucharist by dis-
tributing bread and wine to those at table, declaring the elements to
be his own body and blood; second is where Jesus repeats the
prediction of his own passion and death; third is his passage concerning the apostasy of Judas; fourth is his prediction of the
treachery that was to come from Peter.

The mystery of the Eucharist throws further light on the climate
of the supper. Jesus and the twelve disciples are seated around the
table in a room where many others sit close to them on the floor.
The big crowd outside the house is watching and waiting. The
golden dreams of all are focused on the slightest move that Jesus
makes. When the prayers for Passover begin, the people are swept
up in a wave of enthusiasm (like the earlier crowd on the mountain
near the Lake of Galilee). "Jesus, Son of David," they likely shout,
"Messiah! Messiah!"

Luke is the only evangelist to record in unmistakable terms
how the excitement within the house proved contagious for the
disciples themselves. "Then a jealous dispute broke out [among the
disciples]: who among them should rank highest?" (Luke 22:24).
Sharing the hope of the crowd that Jesus would become a temporal
messiah, they fell to wrangling among themselves over which one of
them in the rosy dawn of final success would merit the largest share
of the spoils second only to the leader.

Jesus rebukes them but in rebuking them he speaks of what is in his heart. What he says turns out to be only a reminder to the disciples, but to the crowd it is a piece of news. "And he said to them 'How I have longed to eat this Passover with you before my death! For I tell you, never again shall I eat it until the time when it finds its fulfillment *in the kingdom of God*' " (Luke 22:15-16). As he had spoken on the mountainside in Galilee, he speaks here of nothing except to assert the love of God and the God of love. John at this point records that Jesus "was to show the full extent of his love" (John 13:1). It is by instituting the sacrament of the Eucharist that Jesus demonstrates his overwhelming desire to remain beyond his death and forever *the inseparable companion of every human being.*

Evening was about to change into night. The crowd understood nothing of his doctrine of love. The only thing coming home to them was that Jesus had denied their expectations. These people felt the same disillusionment and disappointment that had been felt by the people near the Lake of Galilee. In proportion to the intensity of their hopes, their disenchantment soured into hatred. As they saw the issue, Jesus, confronted again with the facts of life, was turning into the same good-for-nothing, weakling, do-nothing man.

Perhaps Judas spoke up for the crowd to remonstrate with Jesus: "Rabbi, you say that God is love. But where is God's love in the harsh realities of life? Does God keep silence in the face of our hardships? We know nothing but his wrath. Rabbi, you say there is nothing more valuable than love. But men crave something more. Men want action, they want it now. It's only human nature to want something practical."

It is difficult to unravel the psychology of Judas. He knew beforehand that his barging-in would not upset the firm resolve of Jesus. But in order to goad himself, in order to punish himself for being one who had followed along until today, he spoke. (The Gospels previously record how Jesus had said that one of the Twelve would betray him; and now there is the scene where Jesus indicates that it is Judas. This narrative, however, is thought to be an interpolation based on Psalm 41. Still, I believe that Judas and the crowd really did argue with Jesus.)

His reply to Judas: "Do quickly what you have to do."

His words are not loaded with hatred for Judas. He knew the suffering of Judas too. Jesus pleaded to be the companion of every wretched soul, of every person subject to pain, and Judas was no exception. But Judas was wanting in insight to these depths in the heart of Jesus. At this word from the master he rose from his seat, exploding in a fit of rage. And immediately, following suit, went all those worthies among the crowd, the ones who were in the supper room. It wasn't Judas storming out alone, for they all stalked out with their feelings of disillusionment, their smashed hopes, their indignation.

Judas is the prototype for those who departed the cenacle, while Peter serves as the prototype for those who stayed behind.

Mixed in the crowd were secret agents of the Sanhedrin who raced directly for the palace of the high priest to report the latest turn of events. Most likely Caiaphas did a little dance of glee on hearing what had happened. For it was only the popular support Jesus found among the visiting pilgrims and the local people that had stymied Caiaphas and the Sanhedrin from attempting to arrest Jesus. Yet once the mob had quit on Jesus, it didn't matter any longer to Caiaphas whether Jesus was or was not a political agitator who might be a threat. The greater danger to Caiaphas now would be for the mass of pilgrim visitors, incensed over the Barabbas incident, to break out in anti-Roman rioting during Passover. But with the animosity of the mob now turned against Jesus, Caiaphas saw immediately that this was the moment to exploit the situation. He called another meeting of the Sanhedrin.

It didn't take long for the crowd to gather around the high priest's palace. Judas stepped forward, and in the presence of the assembled members of the Sanhedrin he promised to be a testifying witness against all the extremist utterances of Jesus; and what is more, he offered to cooperate in apprehending Jesus. Then he accepted the bounty offered to him for his services (Matthew 26:14-15).

There are two passages in the Gospel narrative which throw considerable light on the psychology of Judas. First, when Judas broke from Jesus and emerged from the cenacle, the Gospel of John records: "And it was night." The "night" refers to more than the dark of nighttime. It symbolizes the total isolation in the black mood of self-cruelty that engulfed Judas like some ineluctible quagmire. Surrounded though he was by a crowd of people as he walked to the palace of Caiaphas, still Judas wanted to shout it out that he had no part with the crowd. The mob was all of a kind in reviling Jesus, yet Judas despised them. What is more, he despised himself.

The second revealing passage is the biblical account of how he accepted from Caiaphas the measly reward of thirty pieces of silver Judas was painfully aware that the price of thirty silver coins was an insult to the lifework of Jesus. It didn't amount to a tear from the eye of a sparrow, and he knew it to be the price for which he was selling his own soul as well. He took the paltry sum contemptuously handed to him by the high priest, knowing full well that the price was in line with his own ignoble deed. We can see it before our eyes—the ugly twist to the face of Judas, his mood of self-savagery when he snatches the money. The scathing biblical record of the thirty pieces of silver drips with these vivid impressions of the torment of Judas, the self-hatred of Judas, the isolation of Judas.

He considered how on the following day Jesus would be rejected, jeered at, spat upon by the people. But he also took thought for himself of how until the end of time he, as the traitor, would be rejected, jeered at, spat upon by the whole human race. We don't know to what extent he pondered at that time this strange analogy between the betrayer and the betrayed. If Jesus, however, so much as once crosses the life of any person, that person becomes forever unable to forget.

We will turn our eye once more to the house where the Last Supper is taking place.

After the crowd in frustration had departed on the heels of Judas, a feckless silence no doubt lay hold of those who were left. Peter was the only one on edge. He cries out: "Lord, I am ready to go with you to prison and death" (Luke 22:33).

Jesus brings a wan sort of smile to his sunken eyes. He shakes his head. In loneliness he listens to Peter's outcry, because he feels that not only Peter but the remaining ten disciples, all of them, were going to disown him as Judas had already done.

"No, Peter, I tell you, tonight before the cock crows you will deny me. [Don't say any more.] But for you I have prayed . . . that when you come to yourself, you must lend strength to your brothers" (Luke 22:32).

Jesus was concerned that after his death the Eleven would be threatened in life and limb not only by the Sanhedrin but also by the Passover pilgrims who had transformed their disillusionment into furious hate. "Whoever has a purse had better take it with him, and his pack too; and if he has no sword [to protect himself], let him sell his coat to buy one" (Luke 22:36).

There are a few scholars who draw from these words conclusions about an armed rebellion by Jesus and the disciples. The interpretation is utterly far-fetched, although it does remain that Jesus even at this time expressed detailed concern about how the disciples might be molested later that night after he himself was apprehended.

So it came about that immediately before the feast of Passover the followers of Jesus split in two. It seems to me, however, that the split was rooted in the positive intention of Jesus himself. Even before the event he was well aware that Judas and the rebel faction would be immediately bought off by the Sanhedrin, and as a result he was well aware of the fate that was to befall him.

After Judas and the crowd stormed into the night and away from the last meal of Jesus, the master set to reinforcing the final bond between himself and those who had stayed behind. Nevertheless, he considered his own death as a necessary premise to their bond of union. It was at this juncture that Peter cried out, "Lord, I am ready to go with you, to prison and to death."

But Jesus was familiar with human treachery. In the towns and villages by the Lake of Galilee all kinds of people had come to follow him at first, but by and by people had stoned him and had even attempted to shove him over the precipice of the hill above Nazareth. Many a time with the sick and the lame, with whom he had tried to share the pain, he had come to experience how once their suffering had been relieved, they dropped away and forgot him. Now Judas and the others had left, but Jesus had the foreboding of how even the paltry number of disciples who were good enough to remain in the little house would themselves desert him some few hours hence as the tragedy played itself out.

Yet his own death was the only means to salvage the weakness of the disciples. He conceded that they would remain weak until he was dead, while at the same time he was staking everything on the expectation that his death would fortify his bond of solidarity with them. When Jesus at the last Supper distributed the bread and the cup of wine, using the words which established a connection between these elements and his own body and blood, we can see him urging this bond of union which depended on his dying. The narrative here is not simply a recording of liturgical tradition as some scholars consider it to be. We have to consider what was in the heart of Jesus at the time—his desire to inspire the disciples by sealing with them this bond of union premised on his death. Otherwise, the scene can be written off as an interpolation born of the Hellenized Church under the influence of Paul. The Last Supper was for Jesus a weeding out of his disciples and a dining together in intimate union with those who remained with him.

Having finished the supper, Jesus and his friends went out of the city and headed toward Mount Olivet beyond the walls. Visitors today in Jerusalem can see an ancient staircase excavated in the courtyard of a church. These steps are said to be the only remains of the palace of Caiaphas. Today the steps are almost completely worn away, but it was down these steps that Jesus and the disciples walked on their way to the foot of the Mount of Olives. The lower reaches of the mountain had an area set aside for tombs, and another area was planted with olive trees. Within the olive orchard stood a press to extract the oil of the fruit, hence the name Gethsemane.

Directly opposite from Gethsemane were visible the temple and the city walls. Now it was night, and scattered about on the mountainside were the masses of pilgrims who had come for the Passover beginning the next day, already sound asleep. The gloomy silhouette of lofty city walls and the massive buildings of the temple rose up to challenge the hush of the starlit sky. On reaching the orchard each of the disciples found himself   cozy place to lie beneath the trees. They had no thought for what the Judas-group might be up to after having parted company. It seems that Jesus alone had any foreboding of how the crowd of disillusioned ones might choose to move against him. He went apart from the drowsy unwitting disciples, and he fell to brooding on his own isolation, struggling with his fear of the ordeal soon to fall on him alone.

He had been for several months resolved to die, but the death that pressed upon him now was bitter. Because love made him willing to die, it was certain that death would come to him in miserable and appalling form. It is easy to die for the sake of those who love us. But it was heart-rending to offer his life for people who did not love him in return—for people who did not understand him. An heroic glorious death is easy. But it is most arduous to march to death in the midst of misunderstanding, in the midst of jeers and spittle. He knew that his death would be more wretched and meaner than a dog's.

Luke's Gospel records his cry of anguish in these words: " 'Father, if thou be willing, remove this cup [of suffering] from me: nevertheless not my will, but thine, be done. . . . And being in an agony he prayed more earnestly: and his sweat was as it were great drops of blood falling down to the ground .' "

The disciples on their part were tired out. The unrest of Jesus—was it too much for them? They soon fell sound asleep beneath the trees. I find it hard to understand their falling asleep. Had they no thought of how pressing the situation was, and how Caiaphas would waste no time in moving to arrest Jesus? Or did they relax their guard with the prospect of spending the night quietly by themselves in this familiar gathering place at the foot of Olivet, in contrast to the house of Simon where they had spent the previous few nights?

On the other side there is Caiaphas, who, having called the Sanhedrin into extraordinary session, informed the members of how public opinion had turned against Jesus, how popular support had vanished, and how there would be no rioting by the pilgrims even if Jesus were taken into custody. Rather than being concentrated on the Nazarene, the interest of the rabble might now be turned to freeing the anti-Roman activist Barabbas.

Therefore, how about a plan to petition the governor of Judea to release Barabbas, trading Jesus for him? How about preserving law and order in all Judea and buttressing the power of the Sanhedrin if it cost no more than the life of only one man, Jesus? Caiaphas had advised the council along this line on a former occasion. Now suddenly he put the issue to a vote.

They had to carry out the arrest and the trial in a single quick and decisive action because the Jewish Law forbade any legal proceedings once the week-long festival of Passover had formally commenced.

Immediately the high priest dispatched a squad of temple police to Gethsemane at the foot of Olivet. Of course it was Judas who informed him that Jesus and his friends were there. From among the crowd were some who also trailed along with the posse. The soldiers from the temple guard wore sidearms of billy clubs and swords, and they carried torches as they went out the fortified city gate, dipped into the valley, and headed for Gethsemane.

Meanwhile Jesus was locked in battle with his fear of death, at a spot "about a stone's throw away" from his soundly sleeping friends. In order to become man's eternal companion, in order to demonstrate the reality of the God of love, he himself had to meet death in its most harrowing form. He had to go through every misery and pain that men and women go through, because otherwise he could not truly share in the misery and pain of humankind and because otherwise he couldn't face us to say: "Look, I am at your side. I have suffered like you. Your misery—I understand it; I went through it all myself."

Jesus feared death to the point that "his sweat was as it were great drops of blood falling to the ground." He wanted to say to the disciples: "Please wake up." (One time he did rouse Peter, yet Peter fell sound asleep again.) In the end he caught sight of, against the city wall, the line of torches quietly moving in his direction, even as he intoned the prayer: "Father, if thou be willing, remove this cup from me: nevertheless not my will, but thine, be done."

From the midst of the "great multitude" (Mark 14:43) that invaded the precincts of the olive grove stepped forward Judas Iscariot.

"Rabbi, *shalom*." Peace be with you!

Judas put his hands on both shoulders of Jesus and he kissed him. It was the ordinary form of greeting with the Jews, but on this occasion it was also a signal. The soldiers sprang on Jesus.

No doubt because the scene of Jesus being arrested stayed forever fresh in the memory of the disciples who witnessed it, the Gospel of Mark, based on this memory, carries extraordinary realism in the recording. One of the disciples (John's Gospel specifies Peter) drew a sword and managed to cut off the ear of a man from the temple guard, but Jesus raised his voice and stopped the action. The disciples in panic ran from the orchard; the youngest of them, it is said, wearing nothing but a wide linen cloth next to his skin, managed to slip out of it and ran away stark naked.

Jesus said to the soldiers of the temple guard, "Day after day I was within your reach as I taught in the temple, and you did not lay hands on me."

Jesus knew the situation. He knew that the Sanhedrin, which had not molested him yesterday and the day before, had moved to take him tonight because they needed a body to exchange for Barabbas. At the same time he knew from the circumstances surrounding his apprehension that, regardless of the charges to be brought, he stood there pre-condemned. From this moment forward he had no faith in the equity of the legal proceedings shortly to be set in motion, nor could he conceive of any escape from capital punishment.

Men holding up their torches formed a cordon around Jesus and then returned in the direction of the gloomy city walls that challenged the starlit sky. The arrest had been accomplished all too quickly. Not a single person had come to his help when Jesus was surrounded. The pilgrims were dead asleep in their tents and apparently unaware of any commotion in Gethsemane. But even supposing they had noticed, they would no longer have given a thought to anything like rescuing the haggard emaciated man who had betrayed their hopes.

The disciples themselves, after scrambling pell-mell from the olive grove, were still driven by panic. They were amazed that Jesus had never so much as raised a hand, that he had meekly submitted to being taken away. But even more, they sensed that they themselves were now in dangerous straits. Their panic kept them confused about what was best for them to do. The Sanhedrin, when morning came, was certain to be on the lookout for them as being confederates of Jesus. That's what terrified them.

If we bear in mind this fear of the disciples following the arrest of Jesus, we won't fail to take account of the real background to the famous story of Peter's denial of Jesus at the palace of the high priest, a background distinct from, but in accordance with, the facts as recorded.

Later on I will describe the event in detail, but for the moment I will only say that when the scattered disciples did get together to discuss their plight, they chose Peter to represent them, and that, using as go-between a person known to the high priest, Peter entered the palace to plead for amnesty on behalf of their group. It goes without saying that such a reconstruction of the event is my own hypothesis. Yet, judging from their mood and from their subsequent movements, it is clear that the disciples never were hunted down by the Sanhedrin. That fact makes it possible to imagine a certain deal having been struck between themselves and the Sanhedrin.

So Peter and the others didn't merely forsake Jesus. To put it bluntly, like Judas, they turned traitor on him. The disciples denied Jesus to Caiaphas, who was the high priest and the presiding officer of the Sanhedrin, and they made a promise never again to have any connection with Jesus. In exchange for the promise, they escaped arrest. That's how I see it.

The disciples were that kind of jellyfish. And precisely because they were jellyfish, once they had closed the deal, from their sense of humiliation and pangs of conscience, they fell into hysterical tears. The story of Peter in the palace of Caiaphas denying any acquaintance with Jesus, and then weeping bitterly, symbolizes the sense of remorse felt by the whole band of disciples. (The most vivid account of Peter's act of denial occurs in the Gospel of Mark, which is the earliest of all the Gospels. The other Gospel accounts, because they were written later than Mark, had to emphasize more the dignity of Peter as head of the Church, and they handle his story more gingerly.)

The nincompoops! The jellyfish! The disciples so like ourselves, base and cowardly. Nevertheless, these same disciples after a while became a powerful group of men who flinched not even at martyrdom. How did that come about? The answer provides one of the major themes in the New Testament.

Judas Iscariot, on the other hand, had returned to the palace of Caiaphas in company with the members of the temple guard having Jesus in custody. He attended the trial of Jesus in the palace, very likely as a testifying witness. We see written in Matthew's Gospel that when Jesus received his sentence of death, Judas tried then to return the thirty pieces of silver, saying: "I have betrayed innocent blood." If that is what really occurred, had Judas believed that Jesus would never be sentenced to death? Or had Judas promised to guide the temple police to Gethsemane, provided only that Jesus' life was spared, and now he was appalled at being double crossed by Caiaphas? It was something like that.

Judas had no concern for the money itself. When he saw the figure of the loving Jesus being beaten by everybody, when he saw Jesus spouting blood, he stared at the shift in circumstances in waves of mixed emotion—loathing himself, then excusing himself; hating the master, then loving him.

When sentence of death was passed against Jesus, Judas decided that he himself must also die. Jesus was being insulted and condemned by the people now. But Judas himself would be condemned by the whole human race forever. What Jesus suffered today was for Judas to suffer forever. He could not escape the strange analogy. Judas certainly, at this time, came to know the meaning of Jesus' life. In spite of what the Gospels say of him, without a doubt he did believe in Jesus.

He tried to return the money to Caiaphas but was coldly and flatly rejected. In the high priest's palace he flung down the thirty pieces of silver which he had earlier snatched in his fist, and going out beyond the city walls, there he hanged himself. Peter later says of him that "falling down headlong, he burst asunder in the midst, and all his bowels gushed out." We get a grim picture indeed of the mortal remains of Judas. But may we suppose that even Judas was saved through the merits of Jesus? I favor that opinion, for the reason that, because he felt the parallel between himself and Jesus, he believed in Jesus. And Jesus for his part understood the suffering of Judas. By means of his own death Jesus poured out his love even on the man who betrayed him.

11 MEN WHO SIT IN
JUDGMENT

FINALLY the stage is set for the trial and condemnation of Jesus, to be carried out that very night. But first I should perhaps say a word concerning the number of scholars who have had their troubles with the record of these events as it stands in the Gospels, and something about how certain scholars continue to wrangle even now about the credibility of the New Testament.

One reason for the controversy stems from the rules for judicial procedure among the Jews, where it was the practice to pass no judgment on felonies except in daylight hours, and never to pass an immediate verdict if the public trial had been concluded within a single day. Next, although the Law of the Jews stated that "a unanimous verdict is invalid," yet the Gospels say that the verdict condemning Jesus to death was indeed a unanimous decision. Another source of contention is that the accounts in Matthew and Mark fail to agree on certain details, and the Gospel of John barely touches the interrogation of Jesus by Caiaphas the high priest. And, finally, it is thought that the disciples, at best, knew nothing of what went on at the trial because, having scattered to the four winds, they were not in attendance at the proceedings. Certain scholars, on the other hand, are concerned about the legality of the proceedings, asking whether the entire trial was not irregular.

In spite of their differences, however, they all agree that the trial before the Sanhedrin was rigged from the start to bring off the execution of Jesus, and that the proceedings lacked due process. Of course, there were also present at the trial some men who were not necessarily bent on destroying Jesus—men like Joseph of Arimathea (Luke 23:50-53) and Nicodemus (John 7: 50-52)—yet it does seem that the trial was pushed along with no one appearing to speak for the defense.

If we accept at face value what is recorded in the Synoptic Gospels, the Sanhedrin (with Caiaphas presiding) began the trial by charging Jesus with the crime of arrogant blasphemy against the temple.

It goes without saying that the temple of Jerusalem, the dwelling place of Yahweh, was for the Jews the holiest place on earth. To blaspheme the temple or display any lack of reverence for it was a heinous violation of Jewish Law.

Yet it had been reported that during his stay in Jerusalem Jesus announced to his disciples, when they were praising the grandeur of the temple buildings, that the whole structure was going to crumble: "Not one stone will be left upon another." On another occasion he had said in the hearing of the people, "Destroy this temple, made with human hands, and in three days I will rebuild another." Pouncing on these words, the Sanhedrin savagely grilled the culprit. The temple that Jesus said he would build was of course an edifice of love, in a spiritual sense, and not the material temple. Still the Pharisees and the Saduccees in the Sanhedrin made it out that his claim was so blasphemous that they were constrained to cover their ears to avoid even hearing it.

Maintaining his silence, Jesus answered nothing to his accusers. Even the witnesses called in by the Sanhedrin were contradicting one another when they spoke, and they failed to establish even the minimum corroborated testimonies required for reaching a verdict. Because the council itself could not subvert the Jewish Law, the Sanhedrin had no choice but to dismiss the charge of blasphemy.

Caiaphas was at wit's end. He must find a crime serious enough to merit indicting Jesus, whatever the crime might be. Having bungled the first accusation, he then produced a cleverly loaded question.

He asked the prisoner at the bar: "Art thou the Christ?"

The word "Christ" means "messiah," and messiah was a word with complex connotations. The etymology of "messiah" indicates "one on whom oil has been poured," and the word can therefore be used to denote the "royal sovereign" or "king." The word covered the two meanings of "king" of the Jewish people and spiritual "savior" or the nation. If *messiah* is interpreted in a political sense, it comes to mean the savior who will liberate the suffering Jews from Roman occupation and restore to them their ancient glory as a nation. Consequently, were Jesus to reply that he was indeed the Christ, they could immediately denounce him before Pilate, the governor, for being a political offender. Conversely, should Jesus describe himself as being a spiritual messiah, they could punish him immediately as one who blasphemes God. The question Caiaphas put to Jesus was ingenious and tricky. (Caiaphas had given it some thought and had certainly prepared the question beforehand.)

How did Jesus reply? I think that the Gospel of Luke gives the answer in words probably closer to the facts than in the Gospels of Matthew and Mark.

Jesus perceived the intent behind the loaded question from Caiaphas. He broke his silence, saying:

"If I do tell you so, you will not believe me; and if I in turn ask you a question, you will not answer me, nor will you let me go."

In effect, Jesus said that his trial was a charade, that it was rigged to insure his punishment, that no matter what answer he gave, they would not accept it. Then he admitted that, yes, he was the Savior.

Hearing that, Caiaphas tore his clothes and appealed to the councillors, "What further need have we of witnesses?" His words implied a verdict of guilty, with which the councillors concurred by immediately decreeing the penalty of death. Among the most recent scholars, however, are some who think the Sanhedrin did not actually pass sentence of death until after daybreak.

The sentence of death was handed down, yet strictly speaking, although the residual right of the Sanhedrin to pass such sentence was recognized by Rome, the council had no right of its own to execute the sentence. To carry out the penalty of death they required the consent of Pilate the governor.

The high priest therefore decided to demand from Pilate the execution of Jesus on grounds of his being a felonious anti-Roman agitator. In virtue of this pretext the high priest was then in a position to save face for the Sanhedrin by seeking an exchange of Jesus for Barabbas, a leader of the Zealot party, who was in prison and whose release was sought by the populace.

At the same time, Caiaphas also hoped that Jesus would eventually fade from public memory if he were to die as a felon.

This owlish strategy may have come to Caiaphas by the advice of his father-in-law, the former high priest Annas.

According to the twenty-third chapter in Luke's Gospel, the high priest Caiaphas took all the councillors who were present and marched at their head to Pilate, to dramatize that the verdict of the Sanhedrin was unanimous. Caiaphas knew that the presence of all the councillors would in itself be a demonstration powerful enough to put the governor under pressure.

The official residence, or pretorium, of Pilate was located in a section of Jerusalem close to what is know today as David's Gate, about a seven- or eight-minute walk from the mansion of Caiaphas. The successive Roman governors of Judea did not live permanently in Jerusalem (maintaining their usual residence in Caesarea), but Pilate happened that week to be in Jerusalem, because by custom the governors always came to the "eternal city" for the festival of Passover.

Pilate was of Samnite extraction, from the southeast part of Italy, from which ethnic group had come several conspirators involved in the assassination of Julius Caesar, and there were Samnites currently holding administrative office in the court of the emperor Tiberius. Pilate had arrived at his post in Palestine in the year 26 of the Western calendar, bringing with him his wife Procula, and he held his position for ten years. Having assumed his office, he wasted no time before making an entry into Jerusalem, an occasion on which he aroused the indignation of the Jews by choosing to ignore their religious sensibilities and parading into Jerusalem under

Roman military standards bearing the emperor's graven image.

But in the early morning of the day on which he was apprised of a petition from the high priest Caiaphas and the others in the Sanhedrin, the position of Pilate was obviously changed from what it had been at the time when he first took office. With the overthrow of Sejanus, his powerful patron in Rome, Pilate was left with only his own resources to maintain his authority. Because his office of governor was subject to supervision by the Roman legate of Syria, Pilate was skittish about handing the Jews any cause to lodge complaints against him, and his anxiety for avoiding trouble between himself and the Jews put him at a disadvantage. The extent to which Caiaphas was aware of Pilate's weak position can be gathered from the biblical account of the way in which the Sanhedrin confronted Pilate—with an attitude little short of being insolent.

Pilate held office hours in the morning, in accord with Roman custom.

The Sanhedrin said not a word, of course, about the religious nature of the midnight inquisition carried out in the mansion of Caiaphas only a few hours before, because they intended charging Jesus with being a malefactor in the political order.

A comparison of the three Synoptic Gospels and John shows that John and Luke give more details than do the other two authors in describing the initial phase of the trial before Pilate, and especially in John's Gospel the words of Jesus are quoted at noticeably greater length.

From the questions tossed back and forth between Pilate and the members of the Sanhedrin, we can stitch together the following account from what is recorded in Luke and John.

First of all, the councillors, being religiously observant Jews, were prohibited from entering the house of a Gentile prior to eating the lamb sacrificed at Passover. They sent Jesus alone into the official residence while they remained outside and waited for the governor to come to them. Pilate had no other choice but to go out and inquire the grounds for their accusation. So began the following exchange: (The italics represent citations from Luke, the rest is from John.)

SANHEDRIN:	If he were not a criminal, we should not have brought him before you.
PILATE:	Take him away and try him by your own Law.

SANHEDRIN: We are not allowed to put any man to death.
                    . . . We found this man subverting our nation,
                    opposing the payment of taxes to Caesar and
                    claiming to be the Messiah, a king.

This exchange shows how Pilate, the governor, sensed from
the very beginning that Jesus was not a political offender but was in
violation of the canons of the Jewish religion, which Pilate considered none of his own business; and it shows how reluctant the
governor was to become embroiled in their quarrel. That is why he
could advise the Sanhedrin to try the case by their own Law,
without involving the Roman authority. The Sanhedrin, however,
opposed to any such disposition, answered the governor by insisting
that it most certainly was a political case, and they offered the
governor two charges calling for legal action: (1) that Jesus
encouraged the anti-Roman movement among the populace by
calling himself a messianic king, and (2) that he had forbidden the
payment of taxes to Rome.

Because the Sanhedrin claimed that he was an anti-Roman
agitator, Pilate in his official position could not escape the duty of
questioning Jesus. Should he refuse to do at least that much, the
Sanhedrin might lodge a complaint against Pilate before his superior
officer, the Roman legate in Syria.

In jeopardy between two fires, Pilate had no other choice but to
retreat inside his residence, and there he questioned the captive
Jesus:

PILATE: Are you the king of the Jews?
JESUS: The words are yours, (but) my kingdom does
                 not belong to this world.

Pilate accepted the answer of Jesus, and was still of a mind that
his hunch from the beginning had been correct. He had no interest
in the religious teachings of Jesus, nor could he bring himself to
believe that this exhausted human specimen before him, this
emaciated figure with the sunken eyes, could ever become, like
Barabbas, an obstreperous champion of the anti-Roman activists.

Not the Synoptic Gospels, but only the Gospel of John (with its
more detailed record of the words of Jesus) reports how in answer-
ing Pilate's question Jesus volunteered to say: "My task is to bear
witness to the truth. For this was I born; for this I came into the

world, and all who are not deaf to truth listen to my voice."

By way of reaction to this answer from Jesus, Pilate put all the skepticism of a cynical Roman into his tight-lipped smile: "What is truth?"

That's all he said. He could muster no better reply to the words of Jesus than the retort "What is truth?"—a fact which shows how Pilate, the Roman, was indifferent toward Jesus, or how at most he felt a mild contempt for him; but in no way could Pilate entertain any fear of Jesus being an anti-Roman activist. For the second time Pilate went out into the sunlight, now beginning to grow hot, to face the stubborn members of the Sanhedrin waiting there for him.

"I find no crime in this man," he insisted (Luke 23:4).

As I mentioned earlier, the Sanhedrin for its own part was under pressure to seek the release of Barabbas, in place of whom they wanted to substitute Jesus. To that end they applied the squeeze on Pilate.

SANHEDRIN: His teaching is causing disaffection among the people all through Judea. It started from Galilee and has spread as far as this city.

PILATE: Is this man a Galilean?

On hearing their affirmative answer, the governor adverted to the fact that the tetrarch of Galilee, Herod Antipas, also happened to be in the city, like himself, on account of the Passover.

There was little love to be lost between the governor of Judea and Herod Antipas. And since they held each other in contempt, it is not surprising that it entered Pilate's head to push the troublesome business of Jesus' trial onto the tetrarch of Galilee, whom he despised. (No record of the interrogation of Jesus by Herod appears in John's Gospel, nor in Mark or Matthew either, but only in the Gospel of Luke. Yet I must say that this lone account bears a high degree of verisimilitude.) Declaring that a Galilean had the right to be tried before the ruler of Galilee, Pilate proposed to the Sanhedrin that he "send Jesus over to Herod."

Mindful of how in a previous time Herod had put to death John the Baptist, the councillors grudgingly took up the suggestion. If they succeeded in getting King Herod to endorse their verdict of capital punishment for Jesus, then Pilate the governor would be in no position to rule against it.

The whole Sanhedrin, with Caiaphas in the lead, moved off to the palace of King Herod, not far from the pretorium of Pilate.

There had been a time, in Galilee, when Herod wanted to have a look at Jesus. This same Herod, whose ear had detected the rumor about Jesus being another John the Baptist come to life, was eager to see Jesus for two reasons: one being his superstitious awe, the other his neurotic curiosity. So Herod "was greatly pleased" (Luke 23:8) at this fortuitous opportunity presented by the governor's request that he interrogate Jesus.

It would seem that Jesus himself never had pleasant thoughts about Herod (Luke 13:32). The feelings on both sides were apparent in the palace of Herod, for on this occasion Jesus preserved absolute silence in the presence of the king of Galilee (whom he had previously referred to as "that fox"), and he "made no answer" to the string of questions laid on him by the sickly curiosity of the king. Herod wished to see a miracle from Jesus, but coming to understand that Jesus would not deliver, the king gradually lost his superstitious awe. Free of his neurotic fear, he got the idea of using Jesus as a means for healing the rift between himself and the governor of Judea. He would let the governor see that he, too, had found this fellow to be beneath their official concern. Then, ridiculing Jesus for being a "messiah" without miraculous powers, he added the insult of dressing him in a fool's gaudy costume before sending him back to the governor's pretorium. Since the two found themselves agreeing in their estimate of Jesus, in the words of Luke's Gospel, "they became friends with each other that very day."

As for Pilate himself, while he was annoyed at Herod's sending back this pitiful specimen of a man, at the same time he felt fortified in facing the members of the Sanhedrin with his verdict:

"You brought this man before me on a charge of subversion. But, as you see, I have myself examined him in your presence and found nothing in him to support your charges. No more did Herod, for he has referred him back to us. Clearly he has done nothing to deserve death."

Accordingly, Pilate tried appeasing the councillors by promising merely to "let him off with a flogging." Then he tried another expedient. He would grant Jesus the special pardon that was an established custom for Passover. The "special pardon' consisted in releasing a criminal from prison in connection with the annual festival. It isn't clear just how this custom ever got started, but in any event, by suggesting pardon the governor was trying to exonerate Jesus and to settle the case as peaceably as possible (for Pilate also feared that if he executed him, the friends of Jesus might stir up a violent demonstration).

So ended the first stage of the trial of Jesus before Pilate. But as the noon hour gradually approached, with the rays of the sun growing ever more hot, the situation suddenly changed and entered a second state. What happened was that a crowd of people from the lower city besieged the pretorium of Pilate.

Since the New Testament says nothing either way, we really don't know whether this new crowd of people was a simple mob, or whether it was a demonstration planned in advance by the Sanhedrin. We have already related how on the previous evening the crowd at the Last Supper became disillusioned with Jesus, and how their disillusionment soured into animosity. Perhaps this same crowd now marched on the pretorium of Pilate because they wanted the genuine rebel Barabbas released rather than Jesus with his good-for-nothing talk about love.

Just when Pilate was at the point of saving Jesus by issuing orders for the pardon, the mob surging against the pretorium provided its powerful support for Caiaphas and the councillors to press their demand for the condemnation of Jesus as a political malefactor.

Caiaphas and his associates, fully aware of Pilate's weakness, adapted their tactics by applying pressure at the point where he was most vulnerable. What the governor feared most was any kind of insurrection breaking out during Passover, when it was so easy for something to ignite the explosive nationalism of the Jews. He dreaded any disturbance of law and order in Jerusalem while he was personally present in the city. As I have said many times, after Sejanus (who was in fact the governor's political patron) had himself lost his power, Pilate no longer could afford the show of arrognace which had marked his previous strongarm methods against the Jews. Pilate could display an inflexible and merciless character only so long as he enjoyed support from higher up; but cut loose a man of his character and put him on his own, he will in an instant change from a rat to a mouse. In any event, at this particular time in his career, Pilate's top priority lay in maintaining his rank as governor of Judea, and for that reason it was peace-at-any-price that determined his every move.

Caiaphas and the Sanhedrin members were acutely knowledgeable of Pilate's weakness. The explanation of their sensitivity lies in their own equally precarious position. If the ultra-nationalists and the gang from the Zealot party—all of whom supported Barabbas for his having stirred up an actual incident in the anti-Roman movement—should themselves break out in rioting to effect the deliverance of Barabbas, then the Jewish Sanhedrin might be suppressed by Rome, and Caiaphas and his supporters would stand bereft of political power. Consequently the Sanhedrin needed to obtain the release of Barabbas and to sacrifice Jesus, and then to carry off the Passover celebration without public disorder. On this last point, the interests of Pilate and the Sanhedrin happened to dovetail perfectly.

A superficial reading of the Gospels gives the impression that Pilate tried more than ever to save Jesus, even after the mob had besieged the pretorium late in the morning, but my own idea is a little different. Once he was faced with the mob, Pilate wasted precious few minutes before changing direction. The governor, who had gone so far as to propose exonerating Jesus because he feared the death penalty might stir up an insurrection by the supporters of Jesus, saw immediately that his fears had been groundless and that the better part of prudence would be to release Barabbas instead of Jesus.

Testing his intuition, he asked the crowd assembled in front of the pretorium: "Which do you want me to release as your choice, Barabbas or Jesus called the Messiah?"

Pilate did not pose this question simply because, in the words of Matthew's Gospel, "he knew that the Sanhedrin had handed him over out of mere spite." This time Pilate cared nothing one way or the other about the fate of Jesus; he would rationalize his decision by trying to make this demand for the death penalty appear to represent a general consensus of the Jews. Pilate was playing the politician.

As for the mob, they had no respect for the likes of Jesus. It was the rebel Barabbas, the man of action, who supplied the torch that fired their hopes.

PILATE:	Which of the two do you want me to release for you?
CROWD:	Barabbas. . . .
SANHEDRIN:	If you let this man go, you are no friend to Caesar.
PILATE:	Then what am I to do with Jesus called the Messiah?
CROWD:	Crucify him!

This dialogue, recorded both in the Synoptics and in John, carries all the tension of a drama created for the stage. The councillors strike at the governor's most vulnerable point when they hint that Pilate is no friend of the Roman emperor if he doesn't put Jesus to death. The threat in their voices certainly had its effect on the man who feared more than anything else the loss of his office of governor.

Pilate, for his own part, in order to shift the full responsibility for his execution of Jesus onto the Jews, was now consulting the crowd about even the method to be used in putting Jesus to death. By so doing he was making it impossible later on for the Jewish Sanhedrin to lay false representations against him before his superior officer, the Roman legate in Syria. The pressure was intense, and behind the questions and the answers we can sense the hidden motives operating on both sides.

The crowd demanded crucifixion for Jesus. Perhaps the crowd was suborned by Caiaphas and the Sanhedrin, for crucifixion was the method of punishment employed by Rome, and among the Jews it was not a traditional method of penal execution. I intend to pursue this point in greater detail later on, but the usual method of execution applied by the Jews and the Sanhedrin for *religious dissenters* was not crucifixion, but death by stoning (always bearing in mind that, in the days of Jesus, Rome recognized the residual right of the Sanhedrin to pass a sentence of death but reserved to itself the right to execute such sentences). To cite an example, a man named Stephen, a member of the early Christian Church, was put to death by stoning (Acts of the Apostles 7:57-58) because he was reckoned a heretic in relation to Judaism.

In the case of Jesus, therefore, we cannot skip lightly over the response from the Sanhedrin and from the crowd to "crucify him." In other words, they were demanding the death penalty not for his being a heretic but for being a political offender. Their desire for his execution not by stoning but by crucifixion was simply an attempt to liquidate Jesus not for heterodoxy but for the civil crime of anti-Roman activism.

Why so? I have returned to this point repeatedly. Caiaphas the high priest had it all figured out beforehand. Political adventurers in the end always fade from the people's memory. But some people would ponder in their hearts and continue to discuss a man who preached, as Jesus did, the sort of love which transcends political interest. Jesus was to be erased from Jewish memory. Caiaphas saw Jesus as a threat to the Jewish religion, so it was impossible for the high priest to close his eyes to the teaching of Jesus.

The cross employed by the Romans in executing criminals was commonly any one of three styles: the X-shaped cross was called *crux decussata*, the T-shaped cross was named *crux commissa*, and the+-shaped cross was termed *crux immissa*. Among these three types, most Christians today believe that Jesus was nailed to the *crux immissa*—their opinion based on Matthew 27:37, where it is said that at the top of the cross "they placed the inscription stating his guilt: 'This is Jesus, the King of the Jews,'" but of course no one can be certain.

Condemned criminals were flogged before being fixed to the cross, and sometimes the flogging was done on the way to the place of execution.

After releasing Barabbas from prison, and after following the usual procedure by having Jesus scourged, Pilate left the prisoner in custody of his soldiers. They, in turn, led Jesus to their barracks, where after the whole corps had rallied round, they first removed his clothes and threw a red cape around him, then crowned his head with a species of thorn referred to as *etabu*, which was growing in the barracks' courtyard, and having stuck a reed in his right hand, they had their sport which included all manner of indignities, like spitting on Jesus.

Meanwhile, in accord with the practice in Roman law, Pilate had one of his underlings prepare an inscription to indicate the criminal's offense. He had to keep a record of the crime for the archives, to be forwarded to the Roman emperor. After giving the matter probably only a moment's thought, he decided to specify the criminal charge with these words: "Jesus of Nazareth, the king of the Jews." The governor's choice of words was his retaliation against the Sanhedrin, and against Caiaphas. He intended his chosen words to gall them. He would pay them off for abusing him with threatening words like: "If you let this man go, you are no friend of Caesar."

The title board, written in Hebrew, Greek, and Latin, all three languages, was hung around the neck of Jesus; then Jesus was loaded down with the cross, and bearing the cross on his back he took no more than his first step in the parade through the public streets, when immediately the councillors read the words and took note of Pilate's sarcasm.

This detail appears only in the Gospel of John, but I think John represents the facts: "The Jewish chief priests therefore said to Pilate: 'Do not let your inscription be, king of the Jews, but: He said, I am the king of the Jews.' Pilate replied: 'What I have written, I have written.'"

The place of execution in Jerusalem, where the parade brought Jesus, was called Golgotha (Skull's Mound), to the northwest and just beyond the walls of the city. It was usual for a guard of four soldiers to accompany a *cruciarius* (condemned criminal) to his place of execution, the soldiers being under the command of a centurion, whose responsibility it was to make sure that the condemned actually died on the cross; or, in those instances where the torment unduly dragged itself out, it was then the centurions's job to hasten the condemned man's death with blows from a cudgel.

Making a public spectacle of the criminal by parading him through the streets was intended as a deterrent to others, and therefore the execution party chose the most frequented streets for the spectacle—although today we cannot determine by which route Jesus moved through Jerusalem because the topography of the modern city is quite changed from what it was in ancient times. For the edification of religious pilgrims and tourists a plausible "Via Dolorosa" is marked out in present-day Jerusalem, yet it remains simply impossible for us to identify the original way of the cross, first of all because there are two different theories about the actual location of Pilate's pretorium. As for Golgotha, however, even though not a trace remains of the "skull mound" itself, the locus is pointed out, and archeologists and biblical scholars alike are practically unanimous in accepting it. In ancient times, it is said, the place was a little hill of many rocks with a meager growth of scrub brush.

The hour was midday. They loaded Jesus with the horizontal beam of his cross and made him walk in company with two other convicts—perhaps both of them were insurrectionists involved with Barabbas.

The horizontal of the cross weighed close to ninety pounds and the whole thing would come to more than one hundred and fifty pounds. Jesus had enjoyed not a wink of sleep after being taken into custody in the garden of Gethsemane the previous night. The heavy cross dug into his emaciated shoulders and his skinny arms could not long support the weight.

The streets of Jerusalem were extremely narrow, as they are to this day. Curious onlookers in the narrow streets stared at the procession. The harsh blaze of the noonday sun was enervating, even in the month of April.

12 "INTO THY HANDS, O LORD, I COMMIT MY SPIRIT"

JERUSALEM is like most of the old cities in the Middle East where even today the streets running through the town are winding and narrow and sometimes come to a dead end. The walls that line both sides of a street appear to be stricken with a skin disease, splattered as they are by the slop tossed from inside the houses and by excrement from the sheep and the beasts of burden passing by. The streets through which they paraded Jesus bearing his cross were no doubt much like the streets of present-day Jerusalem—narrow, meandering, and filthy. The heat of Jerusalem near the hour of noon on a day in April is like the noontime heat of Japan during June and the early part of July. Jesus, deprived of sleep and staggering under the weight of the cross, fell to the ground several times, but each time he fell he was forced again to move along, if only at a snail's pace, by the noise of the brutal commands and the lashing whips of the Roman soldiers. Although not everything is detailed in the New

Testament, we do know that Jesus reached the point of exhaustion when we read that somewhere during the parade the Roman soldiers enjoined another man to shoulder the cross, a man by the name of Simon of Cyrene, who happened to be coming in from the countryside.

Perhaps the reason why the parade of exhibition is not described in greater detail is that the disciples themselves never saw it. From the moment of Jesus' arrest in the garden of Gethsemane the disciples, sensing danger to themselves, scattered in all directions like the filaments in a spider web. If they were to wander back into the city, they might be challenged for being companions of Jesus and they could be informed on. That was the scariest part. Possibly Peter and one or another of them went into hiding somewhere close to the city, maybe in the home of Mary and Martha in Bethany, and there they waited for the news to catch up with them.

What Jesus showed the people while being paraded to the place of execution was a figure of non-resistance, feeble and utterly helpless. Not one of the disciples came to assist him; and the crowd, which until only the day before had perked their ears to catch his every word, now went to the other extreme of deluging the powerless man with catcalls and derision. Those members of the Sanhedrin and the Sadducee priests who joined the procession gazed cooly at the goings-on and relished their own satisfaction.

The most striking feature in the text of the passion narrative is the way it dares, without hesitation, to spotlight in front and center stage the feeble and helpless figure of Jesus. On the word of the men who wrote the New Testament, Jesus had previously accomplished any number of marvelous works, powerful deeds like healing the sick and raising the dead, and speaking a message pregnant with wisdom. There had been many signs indicating to the disciples and to the multitudes that Jesus was a prophetic teacher with glowing prospects for his future. It is true that since the end of that summer in Galilee the crowd had turned against him, and there was even that occasion when they tried to kill him by shoving him over the precipice at Nazareth, but even in these circumstances the Gospel writers depicted nothing like this helpless figure of Jesus that appears in the passion narrative. Jesus before the passion was a luminous figure who brought the Gospel (the good news) that "the kingdom of God is at hand," and he was nothing at all like the pathetic *do-nothing* or the *can-do-nothing* who uttered no sign of protest about the whiplashes from the soldiers or the mockery and spittle from the crowd.

Nevertheless, we have come to recognize that concealed in the very fact of Jesus being ineffectual and weak lies the mystery of genuine Christian teaching. The meaning of the resurrection (which we must eventually consider) is unthinkable if separated from the fact of his being ineffectual and weak. A person begins to be a follower of Jesus only by accepting the risk of becoming himself one of the powerless people in this visible world.

Be that as it may, through the April heat of Jerusalem, the parade of the prisoners with their crosses (Jesus and the other two criminals) was finally under way, moving slowly along the dirty narrow streets and approaching the place of execution, an open area close to one of the city gates.

According to John's Gospel, "At the place where he was crucified there was a garden, and in the garden a new tomb, not yet used for burial."

John's Gospel also says: "The place where Jesus was crucified was not far from the city" (John 19:20); and according to the Epistle to the Hebrews, "Jesus therefore ... suffered outside the gate (Hebrews 13:12).

Thus it is well attested that the locus for the execution was close to Jerusalem, on a site which included a garden, and which was known as Golgotha. There is almost complete agreement among archeologists that the present Church of the Holy Sepulchre stands on the spot which since the time of Emperor Constantine has been defined as "the place where Jesus was executed," all of which fits together with what is written in the Gospel of John.

The place in those days was strewn with granite-like boulders and was studded here and there with a few trees and century plants, and it contained a number of graves. The word "garden" in John's Gospel is not to be interpreted as referring to anything like the cultivated plots characteristic of gardens laid out in the Western style. The word refers rather to a piece of land not built up with housing. And the word "mount" signifies nothing more than a slight if bumpy elevation in the ground. Consequently, it is better not to picture the reality of Golgotha being anything like the rather lofty hill depicted by so many artists in the West.

In those days, on arriving at the place of execution, the condemned criminal would be stripped naked (if he had not already lost his clothing in the flogging along the way), or sometimes he was allowed a rag to cover his loins. Next he was laid face up, with both arms stretched along the horizontal beam of the cross he had carried, and the hands were nailed to the beam. After the spikes were driven in, the cross was hoisted by using ropes. Finally, the feet were attached to the cross with *two* spikes. Religious artists often picture the feet of Jesus one on top of the other, transfixed by a single nail; but that is a mistake, for it was usual to have the legs extending down with feet apart.

The Gospel of John records that the Roman soldiers took Jesus' clothing, divided it into four shares, then scrambled for his tunic by casting lots, all of which again conforms with Roman custom. The time was shortly after noon when Jesus was raised on the cross.

It defies the power of words to describe the torment of a prisoner suspended on this gibbet, and yet there were times when men would hang on the cross indefinitely before expiring. In such cases the soldiers would stab the criminal with a spear, or the centurion would hasten death by pounding the prisoner's knees with a hefty club. It was also a custom of the time to give the condemned man a drink of wine laced with bitter myrrh in order to numb his senses before nailing him to the cross. Mark's Gospel says that Jesus refused to drink the wine. He was determined to taste to the ultimate all the anguish and torment possible for human beings.

The crosses of the two political criminals were set up on either side of the cross of Jesus. The worthies from the Sanhedrin who had attached themselves to the execution party from its start now joined the high priest Caiaphas and took their places beneath the cross as witnesses. The Gospels report that the councillors and the other spectators maintained a barrage of taunting insults aimed at Jesus. What is more, even one of the two felons crucified with him began to address him with a similar want of restraint.

Being a novelist, I find myself tremendously interested in the words from the two felons to which biblical scholars seem to give only slight attention.

Supposing their words to be factual—not merely invented by the evangelists for religious apologetics—one of the felons said to Jesus: "Are not you the Messiah? Save yourself, and us."

I don't really know whether these words represent a plea to be rescued from the intolerable torments of a condemned criminal, or whether they were only sarcasm intended to mock Jesus. But if the words were actually a taunt, Jesus answered nothing. I don't know, either, whether to the ear of Jesus the words might not have come like an echo of those testing words which the evil spirit addressed to him long ago in the wilderness of Judea. What remains incontestable is the fact that, in spite of what is reported about his curing the sick and raising the dead to life in Galilee and other places, Jesus displayed on the cross nothing but utter helplessness and weakness. Nowhere does the passion narrative depict Jesus except in this utterly powerless image. The reason is that love, in terms of this world's values, is forever vulnerable and helpless. The two political criminals, insofar as they were both political and criminal, were forever in pursuit of power and its tangible rewards. Politics itself is the quest for material power and worldly success. But Jesus, powerless on the cross, is the symbol of love—nay, the very incarnation of Love.

"Father, forgive them: they do not know what they are doing." These are the words which after a time came from the parched lips of Jesus. He is trying for all his worth to plead the defense of men and women of no love. It isn't that they have received no love; they have simply failed to realize how love operates. They have not yet fully understood the nature of love.

I might say in passing that the words spoken by Jesus during the passion are not restricted only to what we find recorded in the passion narrative. In those days it was not unusual for crucified felons, as long as they could hold out, to speak on various topics to their friends and to their enemies present at the place of execution, so it is most likely that from the agonizing lips of Jesus came other messages and prayers beyond those written in the Gospels. The evangelists selected from all the words that Jesus spoke only those which carried a profound meaning for themselves; and even then, they wrote down no more than the initial words of the utterances reported. That was enough for their purpose, because by citing only the opening phrases of a prayer spoken quietly by Jesus, their contemporaries could easily supply the rest of the prayer, which all of them already knew by heart.

Take for example the famous words of Jesus spoken just before he expired: *Eloi, Eloi, lama sabachthani?* ("My God, my God, why hast thou forsaken me?"), a quotation of the opening verse of Psalm 22, which brief citation was enough to recall for a reader the verses following in that psalm.

According to the Gospels, Jesus was nailed to the cross in the middle of the day—about noon. He drew his last breath at three in the afternoon.

During the three hours of his agony, beyond any power of language to describe, Jesus at first used what remained of his strength to continue speaking at intervals to the people watching him from under the cross. He spoke not only to those below, but he raised his feeble voice also to the felons nailed to their own crosses at his right and left.

It is conceivable that Jesus uttered many more words than what is actually on record in the New Testament, because we must keep in mind (as I said before) that the evangelists give us only snatches or summaries of what Jesus said.

Among the eyewitnesses to his death were members of the Sanhedrin, including the high priest Caiaphas, the Roman soldiers and their centurion, the many spectators who stood watch from further away, among them some women who had faithfully followed Jesus from Galilee to Jerusalem, and also the disciple John. The rest of the inner circle had scattered to the winds, hiding out somewhere in the environs of the city.

Now that their sacrificial victim had been nailed to the cross like some ragged scarecrow, Caiaphas and his cohorts from the Sanhedrin were no longer fearful and not even very much interested. By this time they were assured that, thanks to their strategy, the Passover festival was going to proceed without any undue event and that the prestige of the Sanhedrin was again secure. Very likely most of them returned to the city without even waiting for Jesus to die.

Other spectators kept watching, held by morbid curiosity, as bit by bit the life force of the three prisoners continued to weaken. The spectacle provided for them a splendid sideshow to the main attraction of the festival. Only the women who had followed Jesus waited still for some final miracle as they huddled close to the ground, burying their faces in their hands, crushed by the feeling of despair within their hearts. Their womanly instincts revolted at the insanity that caused a man like this to meet so cruel an end.

During the hours from midday until three o'clock the sun went into hiding behind clouds that formed in the sweltering sky, and the whole area was cast in gloomy shade (Matthew 27:45), yet there was still no hint of any miracle. Time stood still and became itself an eternity, Jesus hanging motionless on the cross, no sign of complaint ever coming from him, until he lost even strength to open his mouth.

At the hour of three, Jesus suddenly raised his sunken head, like a little bird; then he shouted aloud: *Eloi, Eloi, lama sabachthani?* ("My God, my God, why hast thou forsaken me?") The words are the beginning of Psalm 22.

Many have tried to read into these words of Jesus that he was in despair. They are ready to interpret them as words of despondency and complaint, sadness and protest, directed against God the Father for not once making a gesture to rescue him from the cross, for not performing a miracle. And from there these romantic readers attempt to discover the pathos of Jesus and his nobility of heart in the words of pleading that came from him.

I cannot agree. One reason for my disagreeing I have already suggested. The Crucified One gave voice to various prayers at his place of execution, and the text of the prayers he recited did not require a complete transcribing. With only an indication of the opening verse of the prayer, the Jews of that time, who knew the prayer by heart, could easily supply the rest.

Psalm 22 begins with a cry of sadness, "My God, my God, why hast thou forsaken me?" but as the psalmist speaks of how he has been harshly treated, he turns more then to singing the homage of God in words like, 'I will tell of they name. . . . In the midst of the congregation I will praise thee." In brief, Psalm 22 is not at all a song of despair; it is actually a song of praise to the Lord.

After his long period of silence, when suddenly Jesus raised his head and cried out: *Eloi, Eloi, lama sabachthani?* the problem is whether this verse was an expression of despair, or whether Jesus sought the expression of his inner heart in the whole of Psalm 22.

If the first interpretation were correct, how can we reconcile that with the disposition of Jesus when immediately afterward he murmurs in faltering voice a prayerful verse from still another of the psalms: "I thirst," which in turn is followed by words from Psalm 31: "Father, into thy hands I commit my spirit"?

Words like *Lord, I commit my spirit into your hands* are a declaration of absolute trust. To me it is unthinkable to link such absolute trust to an immediately foregoing cry of despair. Consequently the words *Eloi, Eloi, lama sabachthani* indicate that Jesus, after following his disposition of mind through the whole of Psalm 22, then moves on to Psalm 31 and the verse which reads:

> Into thy hands I commit my spirit;
> O Lord, faithful God,
> Thou hast redeemed me.

Having spent his remaining strength speaking to people from the cross, from somewhere then in the depths of hazy consciousness there came to him prayers from the Book of Psalms. He gave voice to these prayers in fragments of speech, waiting for the final moment.

One thing stands beyond dispute in the whole narrative of the passion. It is evident that in this passion narrative—from the moment of his arrest until the time he drew his last breath—Jesus could not, or he did not, perform a single miracle; nor, in turn, did God extend any visible assistance or relief.

If I may be allowed to say it, the narrative shows Jesus to be an utterly helpless, powerless human being. He could not prevail in the least against his adversaries, neither when being grilled by the Sanhedrin, nor at his trial before Pilate, nor against the tidal wave of abuse that came from the soldiers. Faced with rejection by the mob, he could only suffer in silence. Perhaps the disciples, hiding in the environs of Jerusalem, were waiting for a miracle from Jesus to turn the tables before the end, but Jesus did nothing of the kind. Among those present at Golgotha for the execution, looking on Jesus nailed to the cross like a scarecrow, perhaps there actually were a few who expected that God would extend a hand, but it appears that God only left him alone to suffer.

So the passion narrative portrays a feckless image of Jesus. Where is the man who in Galilee and elsewhere had so amazed the people and who had done such wonders to extol the glory of God? Where now was the power that had even raised the dead?

An enormous contrast is evident between Jesus during the passion and Jesus before the passion. One side is Jesus the powerful, the other is Jesus the powerless. The evangelists did not hesitate in their narratives of the passion to write about Jesus being powerless, about Jesus helpless, with love alone continuing to flow from within him, about Jesus worn out, about Jesus exhausted. The quintessence of what Jesus taught us comes home to me (speaking for myself) not so much from that dynamic Jesus in Galilee as from this helpless Jesus on the cross.

Jesus the dynamic, or rather, the Jesus who had been so dynamic—that kind of Jesus, whom the holy Gospels depict in the most resplendent terms, appears in those parts of the Gospels relating to the springtime of his Galilean ministry, when the multitudes crowded about him, when those who listened to his words were vast in number, and when (it seems) he cured the sick one after another and brought relief for every misfortune.

But the resplendent springtime in Galilee was all too brief, and all too quickly it was done and gone. The crowds deserted him— even chased him away—and their behavior made him feel that his very life was in peril. Jesus the wonder-worker became Jesus the feckless. Every time I read in the Gospels about this sudden change, I never fail to be amazed.

Why did these people turn against him? This Jesus, whom they had welcomed with so many cheers—why did they turn to driving him away? And they were not merely forsaking him, not merely deserting him—in the town of Nazareth did they not go so far as attempting even to throw him over a precipice?

There are several possible explanations, and it is hard to condense everything into a few words, but certainly the change began because people were disenchanted. They had looked for *something* from Jesus, but Jesus failed to supply that *something*. Therefore, the people, betrayed in their expectations, turned angry and rejected him.

In what did that *something* consist? We have been looking at it in this life of Jesus, in some small way at least. The men and women in Galilee tried to press him into assuming leadership in the pursuit of their political independence. They tried to set him up as the messiah for their anti-Roman movement. Jesus failed to go along with any such expectation. Quite the contrary, in his message delivered in the Sermon on the Mount—"Blessed are the poor in spirit. . . . Blessed are those who mourn"—Jesus flatly rejected the popular aspirations. Other people, again, were looking only for miracles. When reading stories detailing the numerous miracles in Galilee, we feel the irony of people's search for miracles without understanding what a shabby thing any miracle in itself is when compared to the love that flowed from Jesus like lifeblood from his body. When the miracles failed to go on forever, the crowd grew disenchanted and considered itself betrayed.

From that day forward, in the public's opinion, Jesus changed from wonder-worker to feckless has-been, incapable even of miracles, with nothing to contribute in the world of practical realities. In the end the people were unable to grasp that Jesus was what he was in virture of that very lack of worldly power. Not only people in general, but his own disciples were unable to understand the meaning of the powerless Jesus. Like people in general, the disciples were large in number for a while, until first one of them fell away, then it was two, and finally, as the New Testament says, only a mere handful of men and women remained in his company.

In contrast to the ministry in Galilee with its miracle stories, the passion narrative does nothing if not to describe Jesus' helplessness in the visible world. In the face of derision from the Sanhedrin, against the interrogation from Pilate, in the midst of the outrages from the Roman soldiers and from the crowd, Jesus accomplished nothing and put up no resistance, nor did God ever come to help him. Jesus showed an unmistakable want of power. Smeared with his own sweat and blood, he did nothing but take the cross on his skinny shoulders and walk to his place of execution at Golgotha.

This narrative of the passion, while positively affirming the weakness of Jesus, asks us nevertheless about the *meaning* of that weakness. The passion shows us that being *Jesus* means being weak, by this world's measuring rod.

Jesus at three in the afternoon, still helpless on the cross, finally droops his head. The two messages he had murmured just before he died were: "Father, into thy hands I commit my spirit," and "It is finished."

Three in the afternoon—the time scheduled for vesper prayers to begin in Jerusalem, where from the temple came the wail of the *shofar* to signal the hour of prayer. The wail of the ram's horn trumpet carried as far as the place of execution outside the city limit.

Matthew writes that "at that moment the curtain of the sanctuary was torn in two from top to bottom. There was an earthquake, the rocks split and the graves opened. ... " Luke reports that "there was darkness over the whole land ... while the sun's light failed." Yet the Gospel of Mark, which antedates Matthew and Luke, has no such record. The same is true for the Gospel of John. The fact is that nothing extraordinary happened in any visible way. The sky remained what it had been while Jesus was suffering. The dim rays of the sun, pouring down through breaks between the clouds, showed no sudden change when Jesus breathed his last. The men from the Sanhedrin withdrew, satisfied at their purpose having been achieved; the soldiers with a hefty club cut short the life of one of the felons not yet dead by smashing his shinbones. It was the customary way to end a condemned prisoner's agony.

Since Jesus had already expired, there was no need to do him the favor of hastening death with a cudgel. When one of the soldiers jabbed a hole in his side with the point of a spear, a small amount of blood and water drained from Jesus. That's all there was to it.

To bury an executed criminal in a graveyard was prohibited. Singing a funeral dirge or holding a burial service was not allowed. The body of Jesus would have met an ignoble fate had not a man named Joseph of Arimathea, himself a member of the Sanhedrin, paid a visit to Pilate, seeking permission to remove the body of Jesus. We know very little about the character of Joseph of Arimathea. According to Mark he was a secret sympathizer in spite of belonging to the Sanhedrin, where he presumably was opposed to the verdict of death for Jesus (Luke 23:51).

The body of Jesus was wrapped in a cloth and laid to rest in the rock-hewn sepulcher which belonged to this member of the Sanhedrin. Eyewitnesses to the scene were both Mary of Magdala and the mother of a disciple named Joseph.

Where Mark and Matthew have written that the whole earth shook when Jesus died, and that the high curtain split in two, the evangelists are not recording events which actually happened, but they are rather expressing the lamentation of the disciples and their consternation at the death of Jesus.

To be honest about even the scattered disciples, they had no idea that Jesus' fate would lead to so harrowing an end as this. In their hearts somewhere they were hoping still that he could finally display his power. They still expected that the apparently helpless Jesus would eventually make a stand. When he roused himself, they thought, God could not abandon the cause.

As things turned out, Jesus showed no sign of any power whatsoever. All he did was to die in a way more dreadul and more wretched than most other sinners. The disciples watched and waited for the divine threat of quaking earth or tearing curtains or darkening skies, but the sky in fact retained its normal hue, the dimmed sunbeams showing through breaks in the clouds on an afternoon no different from any other with its continuous stirring of noise from men and women and domestic beasts in the streets of Jerusalem.

Did Jesus therefore accomplish nothing? Was Jesus simply helpless after all? Was God silent? Was the sky merely dull? In the end, was the death of Jesus really no more than the death of any other powerless ineffectual man?

When the disciples first confronted these questions, most of them had nothing better to do than to brood on their own dismay and vanished hopes. They were hiding someplace around Jerusalem, perhaps out by Bethany, from where they watched the master's fate unfold. And when they were finally informed of the way Jesus died completely helpless, they began taking action to go back with drooping heads, each one to his own home town.

The description of the wan disciples who walked to Emmaus, written only in the Gospel of Luke, reveals the dismay and the vanished hopes of all the disciples at that juncture. The lowly village of Emmaus was about seven miles from Jerusalem, and even in our own day the road going out that way must thread a path through the same inhospitable rocky hills where in the dusk of evening the two crestfallen disciples were dragging their feet and "talking with each other about all these things that had happened" (Luke 24:14).

In spite of what they had to say for themselves—"We had been hoping that he was the man to liberate Israel . . . and it is now the third day since all this happened"—for some reason or other they could not rid their hearts of thoughts about Jesus. They could not shake the sadness and remorse they felt for having deserted him. They would have much preferred to believe that feckless Jesus himself was to blame for what they had done; but in spite of all their excusing of self, the person of Jesus contrariwise became more compelling to them in death than in his lifetime.

Jesus helpless in this visible world; Jesus useless to the world—what meaning could be attached to that helplessness and uselessness? The two disciples, still unaware of Jesus' resurrection, had no way of solving the paradox hidden behind this difficult question. Nor could they grasp the relationship between their master, who accomplished nothing in the world by his talk about love, and God himself, who did not visibly come to their master's rescue, even though God in his divine nature had been said to be Love itself.

Yet the pain in their hearts remained—pain in their hearts for having run out on him. They tried to believe that the only thing for them to have done was to clear away from a feckless loser, and yet these same disciples could not eradicate from memory the pain-stricken face of Jesus rejected. It was their inability to forget that compelled them to think seriously about the weakness of Jesus.

13 THE QUESTION

"And when the sabbath was past, Mary Magdalene, and Mary the mother of James, and Salome, had brought sweet spices, that they might come and anoint Jesus. And very early in the morning the first day of the week, they came to the sepulchre at the rising of the sun. And they said among themselves, who shall roll us away the stone from the door of the sepulchre? And when they looked, they saw that the stone was rolled away: for it was very great. And entering into the sepulchre, they saw a young man sitting on the right side, clothed in a long white garment: and they were affrighted. And he saith unto them: Be not affrighted. Ye seek Jesus of Nazareth, which was crucified: he is risen; he is not here: behold the place where they laid him. But go your way, tell his disciples and Peter that he goeth before you into Galilee. . . . And the women went out quickly, and fled from the sepulchre; for they trembled and were amazed: neither said they anything to any man; for they were afraid."

The scene of the resurrection, the pivotal point of the passion narrative and indeed the key to the entire New Testament is described by Mark in the passage quoted here.

Did these events actually take place? Are they historical facts, things that really happened? Or is this a fiction produced by the early Christian Church, perhaps an episode written to inculcate through symbols the undying memory of the Christ?

Probably no one in his or her first contact with the Gospels can read this passage without such questions occurring. Having such a problem in mind, they will proceed to test the account in Mark by comparing it with the other Gospels, and will then discover a certain number of contradictions. For example, in spite of what appears in Mark about the three women, that "neither said they anything to any man; for they were afraid," when it comes to Luke it is on record that the women "returned from the sepulchre, and told all these things unto the (eleven) apostles, and to all the rest. . . . And their words seemed to them as idle tales, and they believed them not. Then arose Peter, and ran unto the sepulchre; and stooping down, he beheld the linen cloths laid by themselves, and departed, wondering in himself at that which was come to pass." And the reader will discover still another testimony to the resurrection, which antedates even the testimony in Mark's Gospel, in one of the Epistles of Paul, where it is reported that Jesus after his death appeared to Cephas, then later to the Twelve.

Is the resurrection an historical fact? Or is it an episode employed to symbolize the deathless memory of the Christ? In order to get our thinking straight on this question, we must begin by considering the disciples themselves, who are reported to be eyewitnesses to what really happened.

As I have said right along, one of the deepest mysteries we encounter in reading the Bible is how it could be that these disciples, who had been cowards, became in the end courageous apostles. How was it that these same cowards, who in the words of Mark "all deserted him and ran away" when Jesus was arrested, afterward "went out and preached everywhere," and not only to the Israelites, for they also undertook distant journeys to many other countries. The question is: How were such men able to endure all manner of persecution and even death?

It is also bluntly recorded in the Bible (Matthew 15:16) how th disciples who went on that earlier journey with Jesus were by no means very discerning listeners to Jesus. It is plainly written that among them were some with overweening worldly ambitions (Mark 10:15-41). There is talk of how even Peter himself fell short of any sympathetic understanding of the final task that Jesus was about to face (Mark 8:33).

Records like these certainly represent something close to the facts, because it is unthinkable that the primitive Church would deliberately invent a tale about such follies occurring in the early days of its own leaders. Even more persuasive is the way in which the four Gospels all relate that the disciples ran away from their beloved master when he was arrested.

In brief, the disciples were a group of people hardly different from the rest of us. Like us, they were happy enough to hear good stories, but they lacked firm convictions and their dispositions were self-centered enough to sacrifice the master to their own gut fear. They were average human beings, strong-minded only in their vanities and worldly ambitions.

To put it gently, poltroons like these possessed no powerful convictions. Therefore, after Jesus died, how did they manage to wake up, to regain their footing, to realize for the first time the true merit of Jesus? How were they able to bring off this interior conversion, changing themselves from mere disciples into apostles?

The New Testament does not discuss the why and how. It only asserts the enigma, then leaves it. Perhaps it intends to leave us a homework problem to solve on our own. To solve this riddle is then the first step toward our considering the resurrection theme.

I'll show you still another problem. Granted that there existed schools of thought which varied one from another among the primitive Christian communities established by the disciples who had previously been such cowards, the fact remains that all the communities were one in accepting the resurrection of Jesus and in proclaiming the Godhead of Jesus as Christ the Savior. Everybody now realizes that the New Testament was written against the background of the theology prevalent in the early Christian Church. Modern biblical scholars, whether they use the method of form-criticism or the method of historical redaction, set their aim at sorting out from the contents of the Gospels what belongs to the Jesus of historical fact and what belongs to the fictitious Jesus born of this theology in the early Christian Church. Well, of course, their efforts have rendered tremendously meritorious service, except that they fail to come up with the key to one momentous problem.

The problem I refer to is the one about why the whole community of the disciples came to recognize the divine nature of Jesus. It is the problem of why one man, who had been so feckless in this world and who had met an utterly miserable death, came to be thought of as Christ the Savior by the same disciples who had deserted him. It is the problem of why the master, who in fact had upset the dreams and hopes of his disciples, was worshipped after his death as the messiah of love by those same disciples.

In the days of Jesus there were in Judea a number of prophets like Jesus each with his own group. Besides the Qumran community in the wilderness of Judea who followed the teacher of righteousness, there were several other baptismal societies, apart from the group on the banks of the Jordan who had made John the Baptist their leader. Among those several groups there never developed any leader who was apotheosized in the manner of Jesus. Of course, various political and social reasons intervene to explain why these different religious movements disappeared one after another, but the failure of these groups to apotheosize their leaders does not in itself explain what happened in the case of Jesus.

The second problem is, therefore, why, among all these prophets, each with his own group of followers, only the religious assembly of the disciples of Jesus managed to survive. It doesn't solve anything to indicate simply that only the Church of Jesus advanced beyond Israel to spread its doctrine among the Gentile nations, whereas the other groups doggedly kept themselves within the confines of the Jewish world.

How did the cowardly disciples come by their sturdy faith after Jesus died? How did a man so ineffectual in this world, who had upset the dreams of his own disciples, come then to be divinized by these same disciples? These two questions forever entangle people who read the Bible, yet the biblical scholars, with their theories of form-criticism or of redactionism, hardly so much as allude to these questions. In other words, they seem to accomplish everything except to answer the basic questions that make the New Testament uniquely what the New Testament is; or they do no more than offer solutions which prove exceedingly fragile on close inspection.

I will cite one example of what I call a fragile solution. In Mark 6:14 occur these words: "One day King Herod, since the name of Jesus had become well known, heard it said that 'John the Baptist is risen from the dead, and that is why the miraculous powers are active in him.'" From these words certain critics began to wonder if the basis of faith in the resurrection is not to be found in the feeling of people in those days that when the power of a dead man appeared to be operating in another man, that in itself constituted a "resurrection"—where people intuitively identified the life of one man with that of the other.

Yet if faith in the resurrection were no more than that, the same kind of faith ought to have been born in case after case, beginning with the group around John the Baptist and going from them to the other prophetic groups. Each of these leaders might be expected to have left his disciples many vivid and stirring memories of himself, and each leader would commit his influence and his final instructions to no one but his own disciples. Then why is it that among all these religious groups, belief in resurrection occurs nowhere else but in the assembly of the disciples of Jesus, and that faith in the resurrection becomes in fact the central point of their doctrine? That's the question, and our original problem remains unsolved.

Certainly their action of deserting Jesus brought the disciples who had saved their own lives a scathing sense of self-reproach, humiliation, and remorse. Some of them with the passing of time would eventually outgrow their queasiness, but for others their feeling of compunction might well have continued to grow ever more deep. The insoluble problem of why that man had to die his miserable death might have stayed with them to gnaw at their hearts.

Cowards, however, can't transform themselves into heroes by means of haunting regrets and riddles. Anyone with a touch of insight into human nature, indeed anyone at all, must agree that remorse and a sense of shame do not infallibly bring about a complete moral change in human character. Without some further and more compelling factor being added, the disciples could not be expected to pull themselves together again, to become inflamed with faith, and to undertake journeys to the lands of the Gentiles. Without something more peremptory being added, the same disciples, so poor in their understanding concerning the master, could not later be expected to arrive at their mature knowledge of the master's doctrine. Without something imperative being added, they could not be expected to apotheosize this man Jesus, the man who had betrayed their own dreams.

But the concept itself of *resurrection*—did the idea even exist in the age of Jesus and his disciples? And if it did exist, what did the concept actually involve?

In reading the New Testament we run into scenes where Jesus guardedly tells his disciples about his doom and then about his resurrection. In each place the written accounts show the disciples either bewildered or without understanding the master's words. Looking at these scenes leads us to think that the very concept of resurrection had not yet permeated the thought patterns of the general run of Jewish people, that the word conveyed no sense of reality.

If we peruse the history of Jewish religion, we see, of course, that the general idea of personal resurrection did have its place in the Judaism of that era. The eschatological book of Ezra contains words which indicate that when the world eventually comes to an end, the wicked will perish, but the good people—those who died loyal to the faith and clinging to their hope in the coming Messiah—will all rise again. The end of the world, the final judgment, and the resurrection of the just are brought together in this one oracle.

In spite of the exegesis of this text concerning a general resurrection that was done by the doctors of the Law, we simply do not know to what extent this doctrine bore any lively sense of reality to the general run of the Jewish people. We do know for certain how their expectation of the Messiah and of the restoration of Israel moved the hearts of the people, but we can only conjecture about the degree to which the people believed in resurrection of the dead.

To back up my argument, I look also, for example, at the passage in the ninth chapter of Mark, which relates a question-and-answer session between Jesus and the disciples. Jesus had revealed a certain mystery to the disciples on that occasion, and then immediately "he enjoined them not to tell anyone what they had seen until the Son of Man had risen from the dead." As for the disciples, they in turn "discussed among themselves what the 'rising from the dead' really meant."

This record demonstrates at a glance that the disciples did not as yet believe in the resurrection of Jesus, and that the idea itself of resurrection was so nebulous that they couldn't find the handle. It is therefore valid for us to consider their perplexity, and their discussing the meaning of this puzzling word.

One of the disciples then recalled the story of Elijah the prophet. Elijah was the character who fought in the reign of King Ahab to preserve the authority of Jewish monotheism against the religion of nature worship infiltrating from the Gentiles of Canaan and Phoenicia. In the time of Jesus the people held Elijah to be the model par excellence of all the Old Testament prophets. The disciples asked Jesus: "Why do the scribes say that Elijah has to come first [before the end of the world]?"

The answer of Jesus merits our careful attention. "Elijah has already come," he replied, "and people worked their will on him."

There is no doubting that in his reply it was John the Baptist whom Jesus had in mind. John the Baptist had been put to death by King Herod, and Jesus was saying that the second coming of Elijah had already been accomplished in the person of John himself.

That being so, does the concept of resurrection mean that we recognize in one magnificent character the reincarnation of some other superb character from a previous era? It appears that this way of thinking was widespread among the ancient Jews, for after this same Elijah himself had disappeared from the earth, the people on catching sight of the prophet Elisha always said: "The spirit of Elijah rests on Elisha."

I have earlier touched on another example, where Mark's Gospel says that after Herod murdered John the Baptist, the king was obsessed by the certainty that Jesus himself might be John's second coming. "For the fame of Jesus had spread. ... But when King Herod heard it, he said, 'This is John raised from the dead. ...'"

Resurrection in this form—the metaphor of a dead man's second coming—had its firm grip on the imagination of the Jews of that time, and on the disciples as well.

Therefore, after the death of Jesus, when the disciples testified that Jesus had risen, were they using "resurrection" in the sense that we have just described? Just as Elijah had returned to life when his spirit and his mission were inherited by John the Baptist, did the convictions and the faith of Jesus come alive again in the disciples themselves—is that why the disciples said that Jesus had risen from the dead?

At first sight this interpretation seems plausible and to the point. Nevertheless, even by accepting it, we have still not solved the riddle of the resurrection of Jesus.

I have asked it over and over: How in the world did these sluggish disciples, who failed to understand the thoughts and feelings of the master during his lifetime, ever manage to become so transformed? How did these cowards, who near the end of Jesus' life had gone to the extreme of deserting him, after the master's death come to possess their own robust moral power and faith?

These why's and how's cannot be answered by appealing to that broad concept of resurrection I have expounded. There is no quarrel about the fact that the disciples became heirs to the convictions and to the faith of Jesus. But the other question remains: Why and how did men, in whom these virtues were almost completely absent, overnight effect their heritage from Jesus? So long as we don't know this why and how, we will not solve the riddle of how Jesus rose from the dead.

First of all, it is clear from reading the New Testament that, following the death of Jesus, his disciples never entertained the idea that they were on an equal footing with Jesus. In other words, never in their dreams did the disciples see themselves as being saviors (Christs) or messiahs. And that is precisely why they could go on to recognize, after the death of Jesus, that he was equal in nature to God himself.

One way of solving the riddle, it seems to me, is to suppose that close on the time of Jesus' death there occurred something electrifying enough by its nature to make the hearts of the disciples do a somersault.

Obviously this electrifying something was simply their assent to the resurrection as a historical fact, exactly as the event is recorded

in the New Testament. But at the same time we can still entertain
doubt as to whether there wasn't something or other in the preceding life of Jesus that could justify some other interpretation of his
rising to life again.

Before seeking that, however, we need to probe still deeper
into what the disciples themselves thought and felt concerning the
death of Jesus.

Shock, confusion, remorse, despair—do these reactions
exhaust the subject of the disciples' attitude regarding the death of
Jesus?

In the first place the disciples never supposed, even in their
dreams, that Jesus would face so pitiable and dreadful a finish. It is
in the Bible that Jesus spoke several times to them concerning his
own sad destiny; and supposing that Jesus really did so speak, it
comes to one of two things for the disciples: either they did not
believe him, or they failed to understand him. If, in fact, the disciples
had understood, they would have been cautious in gadding about
Jerusalem in the company of the master, and they would not have
been so amazed by the treachery of Judas.

The passion narrative neatly portrays their state of amazement
by the way they scattered in flight when they came face to face with
the realities. They naturally had another problem: Why doesn't God
rescue Jesus? Why does God keep silent in spite of the suffering?
Why does God close his eyes to that agonizing death?

The age-old traditions in Judaism told, of course, how God
sent prophets to Israel only to have the prophets rejected, or even
worse to have them persecuted and put to death. The disciples may
have recalled this notion long after the event, but in their consternation at the time, the idea either failed to occur to them, or else they
never got around to applying the notion to Jesus.

Their despondency is dramatized in the episode of the travelers
to Emmaus. Because Jesus proved to be of no practical benefit,
many of his disciples had parted company somewhere along the
line, and even his own relatives treated him like one who contrib-
uted nothing to support the family, while in the towns and villages,
where people at first had rallied round and cocked their ears to
listen, these same people in the end chased him away.

If a few of his disciples still remained, it was because their hearts were captivated by Jesus in spite of his being so utterly without influence in practical affairs, and no doubt also because they nursed some flicker of hope that sooner or later he would choose to show what he really could do.

But with the death of Jesus, even the flicker of hope was extinguished. Their despair at discovering him to be *essentially* weak finally crushed their spirit.

Yet in spite of their dismay and confusion and disappointment, why did some of them stick to Jesus even after his death? Besides the disciples who took off for their homes, like the travelers to Emmaus, why did a certain number of them remain in Jerusalem?

Could it be a voice inside them saying: "Stay put"? After Jesus died, and during the thirty-odd hours until the resurrection, what made these disciples remain behind?

In our analysis of the passion narrative we have followed each step in the trial and the execution of Jesus exactly as it is recorded in the New Testament, but could the disciples' secret be lurking somewhere in the passion narrative without its particulars being exposed?

Their secret goes perhaps like this: Even during the trial of Jesus, how in the world did these intimate disciples manage to be left to themselves in the environs of Jerusalem without being molested? From the Sanhedrin's point of view, they were what we would call "fellow travelers" of Jesus, henchmen to a condemned felon. Call them disciples if you will, but insofar as they were sympathetic to the ideas of Jesus, they were, in the eyes of the Sanhedrin, no more than heretics and rebels. And what is more, their faces were quite well known, because they had been in the close company of Jesus while he moved about the city of Jerusalem to spread his teaching. Peter's recognition and challenge by some women inside the mansion of Caiaphas only proves the point.

Juridically speaking, they, too, were liable to arrest, especially in the garden of Gethsemane, where a character thought to be Peter had actually drawn blood from one of the temple guards.

It seems mighty suspect that these same disciples could hang around the environs of Jerusalem (perhaps in Bethany) for at least the thirty-odd hours following the trial and death of Jesus—and all the more so because, with Jesus being condemned and executed for the crime of being an anti-Roman agitator, their whole company would have been closely watched, not only by the Sanhedrin but also by the governor of Judea. The greater part of them did head for their homes, yet it is strange that to this day no biblical commentator has ever questioned how some of them could remain in hiding while at the same time prominent disciples like Peter and John were openly running to the sepulchre of the dead Jesus (John 20:2).

What is more, when we read the Bible we find nothing in the account of the trial and execution of Jesus to indicate that the priests in the Sanhedrin showed any interest whatsoever in these disciples or moved in any way to hunt them down. Did the priests of the Sanhedrin think it was enough if they arrested only Jesus, and that the others were beneath consideration? Still, it was strange for them to consider it of no importance to capture the disciples, among whom was the one who had drawn blood from a soldier on duty with the temple guard controlled directly by the Sanhedrin.

There are several points between the passion narrative and the resurrection narrative which should cause a careful reader to be confused. Is there no explanation of these points written into the narratives? Or could it be that the elusive answer is slipped into the text in some symbolic form? In the case of the original disciples of Jesus, were certain memories of theirs so painful and so humiliating to themselves that they would avoid even discussing these memories with other people? Or did they talk sparingly, so that the shameful facts found their way into the Bible, but only in the form of some elusive symbol? That's a question to intrigue me.

There is no reason to expect any conclusive answer to be forthcoming in the absence of any more historical materials. I wish the reader, therefore, to appreciate that what I shall say on this particular point is little more than rather bold conjecture.

Here is the way I reconstruct what happened: The secret is revealed symbolically in the story of Peter's denial of Jesus in the mansion of Caiaphas, and also in the story of Barabbas, the political felon who was saved from death by the gift of Jesus in exchange.

First, the story of Peter's denial of Jesus in the mansion of Caiaphas is an event which appears in all three Synoptic Gospels, as well as in John. The four Gospels are at odds on descriptive detail;

the Synoptics record that Peter slipped into the mansion of Caiaphas all by himself, whereas John's Gospel says that still another disciple went with Peter to the mansion. The fourth Gospel further relates that because this other disciple was personally acquainted with the high priest, he asked the woman on duty at the entrance to allow Peter also to come in. Only Peter was accused by this woman and by others of being a confederate of Jesus, while the second disciple was never challenged.

Another variation in detail is that the earliest Gospel, that of Mark, agrees with Matthew in using stronger language than do the Gospels of Luke and John in recording Peter's denial. Matthew and Mark state in so many words that Peter "began to curse and to swear" that he knew nothing of Jesus, but the wording in Luke and John is more restrained. Obviously, compared to the early Gospel of Mark, the later compositions of Luke and John have toned down their choice of words in order to safeguard the position and the dignity of Peter, who was the leader of the early Christian Church. The fact remains, however, that Peter did vehemently deny knowing Jesus.

Granting all that, does this scene represent only the story of Peter, the individual man? The scene is described in such vivid language that no one will deny that it was an actual event, yet I cannot believe that the principal role at that moment was played out by Peter alone. He may very well have gone alone to the mansion of the high priest Caiaphas, but he headed for the mansion to act as delegate for all the other disciples; and after reading the Gospel of John, we can see that it is plausible to suppose that Peter picked up his companion not by free choice, but because he found it necessary to use the good offices of "another disciple, who was known to the high priest," in order to negotiate an understanding with Caiphas. (This seems clear from the fact that the "other disciple" was never challenged at the mansion of the high priest, as though he had no connection whatever with Jesus.)

Can we be satisfied, then, with thinking that those who questioned Peter inside the mansion were merely maids and guards? I would like to think it legitimate to interpret the vague reference to "they" in the Synoptic Gospels as including also the priests who sat in judgment on Jesus. In other words, Peter too, as a representative

of the other disciples, was under judgment by the Sanhedrin, together with Jesus—whereupon, in the presence of the high priests
and the Sanhedrin, Peter "cursed and swore" to his denial of Jesus.

Because Peter was willing to swear his denial of Jesus in such
strong language, some understanding was then worked out between
the Sanhedrin and the disciples' group (again, through the good
offices of the go-between mentioned in the Gospel of John). The
disciples were not to be questioned about any criminal acts, and they
would be immune from any future prosecution. Jesus became the
sacrificial lamb, being made to bear the offenses of all his companions.

"And the Lord turned and looked straight at Peter. Then Peter
remembered the Lord's words. . . . He went outside, and wept
bitterly."

The wailing lamentation was very likely not confined to Peter.
This wailing symbolizes the tempestuous mood of all the disciples
who were in Bethany awaiting the outcome of the business between
Peter and the Sanhedrin. They had avoided arrest and had saved
their hides by deserting Jesus and denying him. So a single line in
the Bible drips with their disconsolate and indescribable grief and
their feelings of shame and self-contempt.

The deal between the disciples and the Sanhedrin is also
portrayed in symbolic form through the episode of the clemency
extended to Barabbas. The name of Barabbas suddenly pops into
the text in the middle of the passion narrative. His antecedents are
not on record.

Barabbas was "a man who had been thrown into prison for an
insurrection started in the city, and for murder." This description in
the Gospel of Luke is all the detail we have, but it does fit in with
Matthew's introduction of "a notorious prisoner, called Barabbas,"
and Mark's explanation that "there was in prison a man called
Barabbas, among some revolutionaries who in their outbreak had
committed murder," while John simply says that "Barabbas was a
robber."

That's all they say.

The facts are of course (as I explained earlier) that this political
felon Barabbas—in those days political offenders were often referred to as "robbers"—was chained in prison, and the Sanhedrin
wanted to substitute Jesus for Barabbas; they needed to consign

Jesus to oblivion as a political felon and not to kill him as an heretical religious reformer.

Nevertheless, in the episode of Barabbas we find a symbolic representation of what in fact occurred for the disciples. Jesus was nailed to the cross as a substitute for Barabbas, and this relationship between Jesus and Barabbas reflects the relation between Jesus and the disciples. We can see that in the clamor of the mob, "Not this man but Barabbas," lies a symbolic parallel to the promise made by the Sanhedrin to spare the disciples when they killed Jesus.

Such is the way I reconstruct what happened. Then if my theory is correct, Jesus was put to death in exchange for the lives of the disciples; Jesus became the lamb of sacrifice that merited continued life for them.

The disciples were spared through dishonorable dealing. But at noontime on the following day, when Jesus moved along the hot narrow streets of Jerusalem toward the place of execution at Golgotha, bearing his onerous cross through jeers and insults from the crowd, the disciples then recognized in the heaviness of his cross the enormity of their own treachery. To their indescribable shame they realized that what drove Jesus to his place of execution was their own bargaining. That Jesus had to die in order to save them was, for the disciples themselves, no mere spiritual point proposed for mental prayer; it was palpable fact. From that moment on, the disciples looked upon Jesus as the one who carried the burden of their sins.

Humiliation, shame, self-contempt, the resulting self-excuses (What else could we do?), and all the other feelings that cowards must live with in order to survive—in that space of thirty-odd hours the disciples chewed on all of them.

There were only two alternatives for men in their situation. One choice was to spurn Jesus completely, to repudiate him, like a traitor who rats on his own comrades, and to squirm and struggle for another path in life. The other choice lay in asking Jesus to forgive them. During these thirty hours and more, they could not bring themselves to opt for either choice. They couldn't decide, nor could they make themselves indifferent to Jesus, nailed to the cross at the place of his execution.

They were imagining how much Jesus hated them, how he was dying angry at them. No hero can be expected to forgive anyone who betrays him.

On account of the public excitement in Jerusalem the disciples had no stomach to appear openly in the city. They were probably not eyewitnesses therefore, to the proceedings at the trial of Jesus, nor to his being paraded through the streets with the cross on his back, nor to his pathetic finish. Yet these doings were naturally the topic of the day in Jerusalem, and the progress of events could be expected to reach the ear of the disciples in full detail.

They imagined that Jesus resented them. They had not only abandoned the master, but in their manner of disowning him they were no better than Judas, who had sold him.

Piece by piece the news began coming in. They learned how Jesus had been taken from the mansion of Caiaphas to the pretorium of Pilate, then moved from there to the palace of King Herod, dragged from one tribunal to another, until finally Pilate caved in to the demands of the Sanhedrin and condemned him to the gibbet of the cross. Eventually they learned how Jesus bore the cross on his back, and how he collapsed several times on his way to the hill of Golgotha.

At that point, what they feared the most was their master's wrath and his curse on them from the cross. The master would call for the vengeance of God against the disciples who had deserted him and betrayed him.

So what would Jesus say from on the cross? The disciples anticipated his words in pregnant terror and remorse.

In our own day we still attach special value to the last words spoken by a person facing death. This was even more true in ancient Judea, a country where it was the custom for condemned criminals in their dying condition to speak out to the bystanders. What would Jesus say? They waited. Then in the afternoon of that same day, when finally they learned of Jesus' last words, those words went beyond their powers of imagination.

"Father, forgive them; for they know not what they do."

"My God, my God, why hast thou forsaken me?"

"Father, into thy hands I commit my spirit."

Three cries from on the cross—three cries which made their shattering impact on the disciples.

Jesus spoke not one angry word against them. Nor did he pray for the wrath of God to fall on them. Instead of calling for their punishment, he asked God to save them.

It was inconceivable to the disciples that such a thing could be. Yet Jesus actually spoke the inconceivable. In the agonizing torment of the cross, in his shadowy state of consciousness, Jesus amiably continued his desperate effort on behalf of those who had deserted and betrayed him. The disciples learned a new lesson about the nature of Jesus.

That's not all. Jesus drew on the last breath within him to murmur the words of David in Psalm 22, and then the words from Psalm 31—acts of complete trust in God, even though God continued to be silent in the face of Jesus' torments, in the face of his death. The words "My God, my God, why hast thou forsaken me?" were definitely not a cry of despair. They were simply the whispered beginning of his prayers of trust, linked to the words: "Into thy hands I commit my spirit." Because the disciples had the words of these psalms at their fingertips, they could see into the heart of Jesus.

Never before had they known a man like this. In their own times there were prophets aplenty, but never one who breathed his last, murmuring words like these. Even among the prophets of old, none showed this degree of love, none showed this much trust in God.

The disciples in fact were amazed and shaken to an extent that defies all verbal description. "Truly this man was a son of God" (Matthew 27:54) was one man's cry of admiration, but it came no less from the lips of the disciples too.

This was the moment for them to begin to understand and to appreciate what Jesus talked about while he was alive. The profound significance of his instructions and his parables had been as though hidden in a mist where the disciples failed to catch the meaning, at the time when they were moving in his company from one wretched town and village to another around the Lake of

Galilee. Now they realized that little by little they would continue to grow in appreciating what Jesus had wished to share with them by his homilies and his enigmatic stories. Hearing only these three utterances from the cross was enough to make them see what it was that Jesus had always been speaking about.

The disciples also found themselves enlightened about how far they had misunderstood the mission of Jesus. They had regarded him as weak in this visible world, as incapable of signs and wonders, as an ineffectual master eventually driven away by the multitudes and eventually abandoned, even by most of his disciples. Now they saw in Jesus, however faintly, what was in truth far more sublime and more enduring than miracles and worldly success.

Beyond the shadow of any doubt, they recalled the fifty-third chapter of the Book of Isaiah:

He had no beauty nor honor;
 we saw him, and his appearance did not attract us.

He was despised, the lowest of men;
 a man of pains, familiar with disease,

One from whom men avert their gaze—
 despised, and we reckoned him as nothing.

But it was our diseases that he bore,
 our pains that he carried, . . .

Until this moment in their lives the disciples had given precious little thought to what lay hidden in the poetic image of the suffering servant which their ancestors recited from the Book of Isaiah. For the disciples themselves, as for the other Jews, the "Messiah" was never anything but a glorious person, possessed of power, full of majesty, the one who was to liberate the territory of Israel, wrenched from their control by the Gentiles, and then to restore the nation's glory. But now, in virtue of the pathetic death of Jesus the "do-nothing," Jesus the "weakling"—and precisely because his death was so wretched—the cry of love coming from Jesus in his dying moments prompted within the disciples' hearts a radical switch in their scale of values.

Is that what Jesus meant? Is this what he was trying to say? Is that how it was? Is that what Jesus was trying to tell us by his brief life on earth? This one lesson only? This was the moment when the disciples began to catch on. From their underhanded deal in denying Jesus to the priests of the Sanhedrin in the house of Caiaphas, their sense of shame, and the dissembling excuses for themselves, the disciples turned to wailing lamentation for their master. All of them, in the manner of Peter, joined him in weeping "bitterly."

They recalled the face and the form of Jesus when he was still alive: the tired sunken eyes, a sad radiance from the deep-set eyes, the pure and gentle gleam in the eyes when they were smiling. He was the man who could accomplish nothing, the man who possessed no power in this visible world. He was thin; he wasn't much. One thing about him, however—he was never known to desert other people if they had trouble. When women were in tears, he stayed by their side. When old folks were lonely, he sat with them quietly. It was nothing miraculous, but the sunken eyes overflowed with love more profound than a miracle. And regarding those who deserted him, those who betrayed him, not a word of resentment came to his lips. No matter what happened, he was the man of sorrows, and he prayed for nothing but their salvation.

That's the whole life of Jesus. It stands out clean and simple, like a single Chinese ideograph brushed on a blank sheet of paper. It was so clean and simple that no one could make sense of it, and no one could produce its like.

There is probably no passage in the whole New Testament which better portrays the disciples' mood than the episode of the travelers to Emmaus.

> Two of them were on their way to a village called Emmaus, which lay about seven miles from Jerusalem, and they were talking together about all those happenings. As they talked and discussed with one another, Jesus himself came up and walked along with them; but something held their eyes from seeing who it was. He asked them, "What is it you are debating as you walk?" They halted, their faces full of gloom, and one, called Cleopas, answered, "Are you the only person staying in Jerusalem not to know what has happened there?"

Emmaus is still a small town, hemmed in by desolate rocky

hills, less than an hour's drive from Jerusalem. In the fading light of the third day since Jesus died (two full days later), a pair of disciples are going back to this town, when along the way somebody else falls in step with them. They seem so woebegone that he asks them why. The two disciples tell him the story of how Jesus had been killed in Jerusalem. They have not yet recognized that their fellow wayfarer is Jesus himself.

What emerges clearly in that evening's touching story is the image of Jesus as *companion*. Before the disciples knew what had happened, I am sure, the vivid feeling was born in them that Jesus, even though he had died, was still very close to them. It was for them no act of abstract meditation; it was a non-metaphorical, tangible realization. Jesus wasn't dead. What is more, they came to sense that Jesus actually spoke to them.

It was beyond the power of mere human nature to return the disciples' cowardly betrayal of him without anger and resentment but with just the opposite, with love for them. At least until that time, they had never in all their living days seen a human being like that. Not only in their own lives, but not once in Jewish history had there ever been such a person even among their prophets and kings. The disciples' amazement was overwhelming. They began to feel that Jesus might still be close by their side. Their state of mind was like the feeling of a child bereaved of its mother, when the child can still feel how the mother, even after her death, always remains close by.

The psychology of the disciples as I have stated the case, is not explicit in the New Testament, but between the lines we cannot escape the feel of it. Even I as a solitary novelist in the Orient can sense that much.

With no more than that, however, we are still at a loss to understand the impact made on the disciples by the resurrection. The reason is that the event referred to as the resurrection can never be thought of by one who is not a believer as being anything but simply preposterous, intrinsically impossible, no more than a chimera or an hallucination. Not even those scholars who devote themselves to the history of the New Testament can offer any corroborative proof, and strictly as historians they can tell us nothing except to say with Bultmann that "Jesus rose from the dead in virtue of [the disciples'] faith."

But we are once again caught in a quandary. The disciples' compunction, which I have portrayed, plus their deep emotional attachment to Jesus for having forgiven them — by itself, this psychological state of theirs does not satisfactorily account for the way in which they overcame all tribulations in devoting the entire remainder of their lives laboring to spread the Gospel. But even being in that frame of mind, cowards like the disciples could not be capable of maintaining their emotional high pitch indefinitely. The passage of time, more often than not, tends to dilute our enthusiasm and causes us to forget our initial resolve. It is more authentic to suppose that what exercised such a commanding control in their lives was not merely their emotional state born of the death of Jesus, their surprise and their consequent fond attachment to him.

In this case, we can't avoid thinking that some kind of electrifying event actually occurred, in some dimension so altogether different as to defy the power of tongue or pen to describe it. Otherwise, they could have continued at best to think of the "ineffectual" Jesus as a man of supreme moral virtue and as a loving person, but they would not have gone on from there to apotheosize him, as they did, by calling him the *Christ, the Son of God*. Other charismatic prophets and religious leaders have been venerated by their followers even after they died, but never has one of them been divinized in the manner of Jesus. The devotees of the Qumran community, suffering religious persecution from the Jewish establishment in Jerusalem, always believed that their own great master, the teacher of righteousness, would return from the dead, and yet they did not proceed to deify the teacher of righteousness. The religious community around John, especially his close disciples, never ceased to reverence the Baptist after he was murdered by Herod Antipas, but they did not believe in his personal resurrection. It was rather that certain ones discovered the mold of John the Baptist reflected in the living Jesus.

Then why uniquely did Jesus come to be worshiped as God within the early Christian Church? It is certainly a fact, as most present-day biblical scholars say, that Jesus was proclaimed to be God in the *kerygma* (the original proclamation of Christian faith) preached by the disciples, but that is not the problem. The question is rather: did the disciples come to believe in Jesus as being the Son of God?

The earliest written testimonial to the resurrection appears not in the Gospel texts, but in an Epistle of St. Paul, but that in itself is no reason for saying that the Gospel record is less factually reliable than the words of Paul. We are nearly overwhelmed by the self-assurance which pervades the Gospels and the Epistles of Paul concerning the resurrection of Jesus. Regarding other miracles in the life of Jesus, the Gospel record is soft, compared to the resurrection. The New Testament writers merely collected miracle stories about Jesus that had sprung up in different places, and they wove these folktales into the text of the Gospels. But the story of the resurrection isn't like that. The style of Mark, the earliest evangelist, endows the uncanny event with reality, and the other New Testament writers insist on it invariably.

"Now if this is what we proclaim, that Christ was raised from the dead, how can some of you say there is no resurrection of the dead? . . . And if Christ was not raised, then our Gospel is null and void, and so is your faith; and we turn out to be lying witnesses for God, because we bore witness that he raised Christ to life. . . . " (1 Corinthians 15).

Their absolute self-confidence, their unshakable certitude, dumbfounds us like nothing else. Whence comes their self-confidence and their certitude? If we are to suppose that the whole event is less than factual. . . .

We who were not eyewitnesses to the resurrection of Jesus wonder about the questions I have posed. How did the disciples regain their footing? Why did the disciples continue to insist on the factuality of anything so preposterous as the resurrection, an idea ridiculed even by the people of their own times? It's easy enough to accuse the disciples of being hucksters of mystical visions, or victims of mass hypnosis, except that we have not a shred of evidence to corroborate the charge. The mystery unyieldingly bends its weight against our hearts.

The Gospel of Mark, the earliest one in the Bible, comes to a close in verse 8 of its final chapter by merely noting the fact that the body of Jesus had disappeared from the sepulcher as if by magic. Nothing more nor less, the end comes in verse 8. Early in the morning of the second day after Jesus died, three women had set out for the burial vault to embalm the remains of Jesus with perfumes. The hour was about the time of sunrise. Of all things, the stone slab which closed the entrance to the vault had been rolled away. The corpse was gone, but a lone young man was seated inside. "Then the women went out and ran away from the tomb, beside themselves with terror. They said nothing to anybody, for they were afraid."

These words are the end to the Gospel of Mark; scholars agree that what comes after verse 8 is an appendix added by somebody else. The recent painstaking research by Campenhausen has corroborated the historical authenticity of the empty tomb, but we can well understand, even without waiting for such research, how the Bible splendidly records that a rumor had been current among the Jews of the time about how the disciples had stolen the body (Matthew 28: 13-15); and we can sympathize with Mary of Magdala for having imagined that the caretaker at the graveyard had hauled the corpse away, for her story also is in the Gospel of John.

In any event, we are compelled to focus our attention on this last line of Mark's Gospel, which brings the entire story to a close on a rather startling note. This finale to the earliest Gospel makes it understandable that the disciples, hiding out in the vicinity of Jerusalem, experienced from the incident of the empty sepulcher a shock to match the shock experienced by the women. The disciples had been affected emotionally by the death of Jesus, but with this new turn of events they came face to face with a different world entirely.

If we grant, merely for the sake of discussion, that the incident of the empty sepulcher is fiction, when we then come to consider the questions I previously raised, we are forced to believe that what did hit the disciples was some other amazing event, some event different in kind yet of equal force in its electrifying intensity. At least, logic impels us to conclude that, whatever it was that might have happened, it was enough to change the "powerless' Jesus in the hearts of the disciples into the "all-powerful" image of Jesus. And then we are constrained to suppose that this other event, whatever its nature, was enough to also persuade the disciples that the *resurrection* of Jesus was a *fact*.

The carpenter who grew up in the back country of a weak nation was in his brief career an other-worldly sort of teacher whom in the end not even his own disciples could appreciate. Not until after his death were they able to grasp what kind of person he really was. For all I know, there may well be an analogy here between their inability to understand Jesus during his lifetime and our own inability to understand the whole mystery of human life. For Jesus represents all humanity. Furthermore, just as we, while we live in this world, cannot understand the ways of God, so Jesus himself was inscrutable for the disciples. His whole life embraced the simplicity of living only for love, and because he lived for love alone, in the eyes of his disciples he seemed to be ineffectual. His death was required before the disciples could raise the veil and see into what lay hidden behind the weakness.

Many readers, on reaching the end of this book, will feel disturbed about why I have omitted (albeit reluctantly) many Gospel scenes and passages familiar to everyone. For example, I did not mention the nativity of Jesus in Bethlehem, nor did I discourse on the date of his birth.

Whether or not it was in Bethlehem that Jesus was born is dubious. First of all, the oldest of the Gospels, that of Mark, says nothing about it, and Matthew and Luke alone relate the story. Many scholars think that the Bethlehem nativity stories in the Gospels of Matthew and Luke are compositions based on words from the Old Testament book of Micah:

But you, O Bethlehem Ephrathah,
   who are little to be among the clans of Judah,

From you shall come forth for me
   one who is to be ruler in Israel.

In the opinion of certain scholars, Bethlehem in the minds of the evangelists was the promised birthplace of the Messiah, and so they wrote of Jesus that he was born there.

All the same, and I have said it again and again, my own position remains what I have already set forth in drawing a distinction between a fact and a truth in the Bible. In this case too, the

Bethlehem nativity might not be a *fact*, but for me it is the *truth*. Why is it true? Because in the long course of human history there have been innumerable human hearts that have ached with need for the little town of Bethlehem. Because in their hearts Bethlehem has continued to be revered as the purest and the most innocent place on God's earth. Because on Christmas night untold numbers of children have thought about Bethlehem, and the memory remains somewhere in their hearts for the rest of their lives. As all mankind has craved the reality of Bethlehem, so also did the authors of the New Testament crave it. The birth of Jesus in Bethlehem may not have been a fact for them, but it was truth for their souls. As for us, when we read the New Testament we cannot bring ourselves to deny what many present-day commentators have denied—that what might not be an historical fact can still be truth for our souls. The human condition is not to be circumscribed by tangible facts. The important point about my own position is that, even if I failed to include the story of Bethlehem in this book, I do recognize the truth of Bethlehem; it is an integral part of that true world which the souls of human beings have craved.

I need not say that not for a moment do I consider this bird's-eye view of the life of Jesus to have encompassed the totality of Jesus himself. Each one of us thinks about Jesus according to the way that this one man reflects our life. There will always be at least something impenetrably mysterious, and there will always be a certain riddle about the life of this man as he reflects our own individual lives. I think that in my remaining lifetime I would like to write once more my life of Jesus, writing it from my own further accumulation of life experience. And when I finish it, I still shall not have rid myself of the urge to take my writing brush for yet again another life of Jesus.